Knowledge of Language

Knowledge of Language

by

DAVID E. COOPER M.A., B.Phil. (Oxon.).
Reader in Philosophy, University of Surrey.

LONDON. PRISM PRESS
NEW YORK. HUMANITIES PRESS INC.

Published simultaneously 1975
in Great Britain by

Prism Press
Stable Court
Chalmington
Dorchester
Dorset

in The United States of America by
Humanities Press Inc.
Atlantic Highlands
New Jersey 07716

G.B.   ISBN 0 904727 01 7 Cloth
         ISBN 0 904727 02 5 Paper

U.S.A.   ISBN 0 - 391 - 00382 - 8 Cloth
         ISBN 0 - 391 - 00383 - 6 Paper

Printed in Great Britain by
Unwin Brothers Limited The Gresham Press Old Woking, Surrey.

Contents

Preface

A student of mine recently showed me an article on the mating behaviour of two birds — sparrows, I think. The behaviour was analysed as a sequence of semantic constituents which formed a particular transform of an underlying code universal in all mating behaviour. The terms are taken, of course, from the theory of generative transformational grammar; and the analysis gives some indication of the remarkable influence that theory has had since its inception. Indeed whatever the influence on ornithology, there is no doubt that generative grammar has had a remarkable impact upon psychology and philosophy. Were it not such a mouthful, a suitable sub-title for this book could be 'A critique of the presuppositions of current psycholinguistic theory'. For, certainly, doctrines stemming from generative grammatical theory have come to dominate psycholinguistic research in recent years. Philosophers, to their credit, have been less hasty to embrace these doctrines, though support for them is far from lacking. It is surprising, given the influence of these doctrines, that no philosopher has undertaken a large-scale examination of them — at least, not a critical examination. It is the aim of this book to provide such an examination.

I have written on these matters twice before (1972, 1973[a] chapter 6). Readers who have encountered these previous pieces may find tensions between them and the present work; they may even wonder if all can have come from the same pen. The fact is that I was far more sympathetic, especially in my previous book, to the psychological and philosophical ideas of Chomsky and his followers than I am now. I mention this for the benefit of readers who, out of misplaced charity, might otherwise prefer to think that they have misunderstood me than to think I really have contradicted my earlier views.

This book is about our knowledge and understanding of language, and more especially, about certain influential views on these matters. I should hope, though, that my discussion might have wider bearings. The psycholinguistic doctrines examined are, in many respects, similar to doctrines found in other areas of psychology — for example, to the cognitive, developmental theories of Piaget and Bruner. To that extent, my sub-title might have been 'A critique of. the presuppositions of current cognitive psychology'.

Chapter 1

The New Rationalism

It is with Book 1, 'Of Innate Ideas', that Locke begins his long critique of rationalism. The reason is not obscure. If rationalism, by a crude characterization, is the doctrine that there is knowledge not derived from experience then the demonstration of knowledge possessed at birth would seem to rule out a rival empiricism. It would, at any rate, unless we find some appeal in Platonic 'recollection' or Mr. Ron Hubbard's experiences in the womb. We shall follow Locke's order in looking at that set of philosophical and psychological doctrines, engendered by reflections on grammar, which is associated with the work of Chomsky and his followers. For Chomsky writes that his conclusions are 'fully in accordance with the doctrine of innate ideas' (1967 : p. 10). It is this resurrection of an innateness hypothesis that, for philosophers and psycholinguists alike, has been the most startling of these conclusions.

In fact, it is easy to exaggerate the affinity between this new innateness hypothesis and traditional views, and Chomsky, as I have tried to show elsewhere (1972), does just that. For one thing, there is no such doctrine as *the* doctrine of innate ideas among earlier thinkers. No two rationalists, and no one rationalist at different times, agreed on either the content or form of our innate knowledge. Descartes, for instance, insists at one point that all our ideas, even those of colours, are innate; but, at another, that only certain ideas, *God* for example, are. In one place, he argues that innate ideas exist only in the form of our predispositions to acquire them, but elsewhere they are made to sound very 'actual' indeed.[1] There was even less agreement on what constituted relevant arguments for innate ideas. For some it was the universal assent given to the presence of such ideas, while for others it was the 'remoteness' of these ideas from anything presented to the senses. So it is scarcely clear what Chomsky takes his own conclusions to be 'fully in accordance with'. One thing is fairly certain; namely that the motives of the new innatists are different from those of the old. The earlier hypotheses stemmed, essentially, from a concern with the status of various propositions men were taken to know. The status of these propositions — especially their status as general or necessary truths — ruled out, so it was argued, the possibility of their having entered our field of knowledge through experience. 'Experience', wrote Leibniz, 'never assures us of a perfect universality, and still less of necessity' (p. 22). The new innatists display no similar concern with the status, or logical form, of items in our stock of knowledge. The principles of 'universal grammar', for instance, which are said to be known innately, are not necessary ones. At any rate, there is no great difficulty in imagining languages which do not incorporate them.[2] Before we look at contemporary motives, though, it is worth mentioning that Chomsky's views, while they are not directly concerned with the logical status of innate propositions, do have importance in this connection — ironically perhaps. For the typical empiricist rejoinder to the rationalists' account of our knowledge of necessary truths in terms of its innateness has been that these truths are generated by language; that, for example, they are definitional truths. But Chomsky's thesis is that language itself rests upon a rich stock of innate principles and ideas. If he is right, the empiricist's rejoinder acts like a boomerang. It kills off some of our innate ideas only to return with a whole lot more. Necessary truths may be analytic, but our grasp of analyticity, as a phenomenon of language, will presuppose a prior grasp of innate principles. If further reason were required for examining Chomsky's views, this result would provide it.

The new innateness hypothesis is urged on two broad grounds. First, it is called in to explain the alleged existence of certain features common to all languages, or to the grammars for all languages. If these linguistic universals cannot be accounted for by alternative proposals — such as that all languages derive historically from an original prototype — then, so it is argued, we must appeal to men's common, human, innate intellectual make-up. For some commentators, this is the crucial argument; but I doubt that this is so and will not be returning to the topic of linguistic universals until chapter 9.[3] More crucial is a second kind of argument to the effect that a person's knowledge of his language is such that it could not have been acquired by him were he not innately acquainted with various principles and forms of grammar. There is, writes Chomsky

> little hope that much of the structure of the language can be learned by an organism initially uninformed as to its general character (1965 : p. 58).

To this kind of argument we shall shortly return.

Although Chomsky and his followers refer to innate knowledge, neither the term 'knowledge', nor the term 'innate', are especially crucial in the theory. 'Innate', I take it, refers to what is present at birth. But it is not essential to the new innateness hypothesis, nor to older views, that the knowledge, ideas, or whatever in question, should be present at birth rather than at two weeks or two years. What is essential is that the knowledge or ideas should not have emerged in a way explicable in terms of experience. So one might prefer the term 'native' to 'innate'. What is native to a species or sub-species may be innate, but like bass voices and beards among male human beings this is not, fortunately, always so. From now on, however, I shall use 'innate' to mean innate or native. Nor, for our purposes, is it essential that the innate component should take the form of *knowledge*. It is quite enough that the child be 'initially informed', or that he makes various 'assumptions' prior to acquiring language, or that he 'hypothesizes' about the nature of his language. I do not deny that it would be interesting to ask whether what is innate, if anything, takes the form of knowledge rather than belief, assumption, or hypothesizing. It's just that I am more concerned with the fundamental question of whether any of these characterizations are sensible or true.

Some commentators want to go further than I have and to insist that it is not essential to Chomsky's thesis that the innate component be described in any of these epistemic terms; that the essence of it is captured by speaking of innate predispositions to acquire language, or of special inborn brain structures.[4] Well, what you consider essential to a thesis will depend upon your particular interest in it, so perhaps psycholinguists, with their specialisation, need not bother themselves with the niceties of how, precisely, to describe the innate component. But these niceties are the stuff of philosophy, and we cannot dismiss so lightly the question of whether the component is describable in epistemic terms. Further, the cavalier attitude towards this question rather presupposes that we know what we are talking about in preferring to speak of innate predispositions rather than innate knowledge, or of an inborn faculty for learning rather than innate assumptions or beliefs — but this, to say the least, is optimistic. Incidentally, I do not think that Chomsky's views would lose all philosophical fascination were we to opt for speaking only of predispositions and the like. Locke and Hume gave the impression that once the rationalist retreats to dispositional accounts of innate knowledge, he is saying something trivial and quite in keeping with empiricism.[5] But on various reasonable interpretations of 'empiricism' this is not so. We return to this in chapters 9 and 10.

There's one more point to make about innateness at this stage. It is sometimes said that the existence of innate knowledge or ideas can be ruled out as absurd, as conceptually and not empirically impossible. The trouble I find with this claim revolves not so much around 'innate' as around 'conceptual' and 'empirical'. If the claim is taken to mean that there are no imaginable circumstances under which it would be reasonable to describe somebody as innately knowing various truths, then it is mistaken. If Frankenstein's monster were, within seconds of its galvanization, to discourse intelligently on politics and geometry, to make assertions and defend them, to point out mistakes in its opponents' views, and so on, I could see no good reason for denying that it knows various things and that, since it has had no experiences whatever, it knows these things innately. It might be replied that the monster can not *know* anything, because it is not justified in its assertions and criticisms. The answer is partly that we are not concerned with knowledge as contrasted with belief, assumption, and the like; and partly that the behaviour of such a monster would be too abnormal for the 'justification' clause to have any obvious application.[6] (Some of the remarks in the last section of chapter 4 bear on this question). Does this mean, then, that the existence of innate knowledge is a purely empirical issue. Not if this implies that we can decide whether actual children have it by simply going out and taking a look at them. Actual children do not discourse eruditely upon politics, geometry, or anything else within a few seconds of their birth. We know that much, and a good deal more. What we do not know is whether what actual children do in fact do qualifies them as possessors of innate knowledge. That the extraordinary behaviour of an extraordinary monster plainly makes it sensible to talk of its innate knowledge does not tell us if the normal behaviour of normal children makes it sensible to talk of theirs. The ability to imagine strange creatures with innate knowledge does not relieve us of thinking further about the criteria for such knowledge. How unlike the monster's behaviour can the child's become before the ascription of innate knowledge becomes perverse? How crucial to the ascription is a creature's ability to discourse intelligently? These, if you like, are conceptual questions.

Like Locke, I began with innateness — for there we find the single most startling aspect of Chomsky's thought. But, unlike Locke, I shall spend little time in direct discussion of this topic. I said earlier that the new innateness hypothesis stems, primarily, from a certain view about what it is to know a language. And it is this view, and the general notion of knowledge of language, which will be our main concern. For the question 'What is it to know a language?' is, I take it, an important one quite apart from any innatist implications an answer to it might have. Indeed, if you will forgive a possible inflation of the importance of my chosen topic, I would suggest that in the competing answers to this question one sees a major divide in contemporary philosophy; a divide that is, however, but an extension of the time-honoured one between rationalism and empiricism. Naturally, one sees the extension of that debate in answers to other questions as well. But it is in the answers to our question that the polarization has been most marked in very recent philosophy. Whether this simply reflects philosophical fashion or signifies the overriding importance of questions about language, I do not judge. Let me add, in connection with innateness, that if your main interest lies in that direction then it will certainly be catered for in the examination of the more general issues. To the extent that the relevant views of knowing a language are discredited, then to that extent the main prop is taken from beneath the new innateness hypothesis.

It would be impossible, naturally, to understand the philosophical and psychological doctrines in question without some grasp of the theory of language from which they have flowed. So I begin with a sketch of this theory, a sketch of Generative Transformational Grammar. What follows is a highly simplified sketch which is meant more as a reminder to those with some acquaintance with the theory than an introduction to those with none.[7] (I might add, too, that the terminology I employ is just one out of many found in the literature).

What is a grammar of a language, in Chomsky's wide sense of 'grammar'? One sort of answer would consist in specifying the various components in a grammar which, in Chomsky's system, are the 'syntactic' (or 'grammatical' in a narrower and traditional sense), the 'semantic', and the 'phonological'. However, are these distinctions sharp or real, particularly the one between syntax and semantics? Is it the job of the syntactic or the semantic component to show what is wrong with 'John frightens sincerity'? To some extent the decision is arbitrary. By utilizing a syntactic sub-category of Abstract Noun and by placing restrictions on what verbs can combine with such nouns, the above sentence can be proscribed by the syntactic component. But if one were to employ the global syntactic category of Noun, treating the abstract notions expressed by some nouns as part of their meaning, then the syntactic rules governing the behaviour of nouns in general will not suffice to outlaw the sentence, a job which will be delegated to the semantic component. This issue, while it is important, will not delay us.[8]

A different sort of answer to the question would consist in specifying the aims of a grammar of a language. A minimal ideal is that the syntactic component should 'generate' all and only the well-formed sentences of the language, for which the other components would then provide all and only the proper semantic and phonetic 'interpretations'. Again, queries arise. The so-called 'Generative Semanticists' have objected to the apparent pride of place this view gives to syntax as the 'generator' of sentences for the other components to 'interpret'. The conservative objection is that it will not always be possible, economically, to permit well-formed, and block ill-formed, sentences without taking various semantic aspects into account. For example, the syntactic behaviour of certain verbs may depend upon what is *presupposed* when they are used. The radical objection is that Chomsky has completely reversed the proper order of priority; that, in effect, the syntactic component should serve a purely interpretive role in providing forms for the 'messages' generated by the semantic component. Even assuming the issue here is a genuine one,[9] it is not one that will concern us. Of course, the aim of generating all and only well-formed sentences of the language is an ideal one. For one thing, it will not be clear over a whole range of cases whether sentences are well- or ill-formed. Native speakers may not agree, and anyway it is not clear what they would be agreeing about. The more realizable aim is to generate many sentences that are obviously well-formed, to block many that are obviously ill-formed, and let the grammar constructed on this basis decide on the marginal cases. We will return to the kind of evidence or criteria for a grammar at various places in this book.

A second minimal aim for the syntactic component is to provide the means for representing the structure of sentences in maximally revealing ways. This will require classification

7

and labelling of categories, of various levels, to which constituents in sentences belong. This, I suppose, is what we used to call 'parsing' at school.

Another type of answer to the question will describe the means by which these minimal aims are to be achieved. Since the number of well-formed sentences constructible in a natural language is indefinitely, perhaps infinitely, large, the syntax will employ rules, of a recursive nature, for generating the sentences. The rules will utilize symbols having reference to various syntactic categories, such as S (sentence), NP (noun-phrase), Det. (determiner), and so on. These rules, by telling us how symbols may be replaced by other symbols, will generate strings of morphemes, or at any rate, strings of 'grammatical formatives' which can be replaced by morphemes of the appropriate grammatical kinds after consultation of a 'lexicon'. The derivation of a string in accordance with the rules will be a 'phrase marker', which is representable in a variety of ways, by tree-diagrams for example. So, given such rules as

    S   → NP + VP
    NP → Det. + N
    VP → V + NP

(where '→' means 'may be rewritten as'),
together with lexical information to the effect that 'the' is a determiner, 'dog' and 'cat' are nouns, and 'eats' a form of a verb, we shall be able to derive the sentence 'The dog eats the cat'. The phrase marker for the sentence might be:

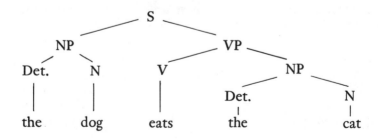

As the diagram suggests, the phrase marker drawn up in accordance with the rules serves to achieve the second of the minimal aims, that of representing the structure of a sentence. Included in the information that can be read off are: the sentence is composed of a noun-phrase and a verb-phrase; the verb-phrase is composed of a verb and a noun-phrase, the noun-phrases are composed of a determiner and a noun.

It might be possible to construct a grammar for a language in which all the rules were like the above 'rewrite' or 'phrase structure' rules, in which each sentence was provided with a single phrase marker like the one represented in the diagram. Such a grammar is usually referred to as a 'phrase structure grammar'. But Chomsky's famous contribution to syntactic theory is to have shown the need, allegedly, for rules of a different type, and hence for a grammar of a different type. Consider the following pairs of sentences:

1 (a) He called up his friend
  (b) He called his friend up
2 (a) He looked up the number
  (b) He looked the number up
3 (a) He hauled in the boat
  (b) He hauled the boat in

These illustrate an apparently general relationship holding between sentences containing verbs composed of a stem and moveable particle. Such a general relationship ought, one feels, to be captured by a rule. The rule might be:

$$NP + v + part. + NP \rightarrow NP + v + NP + part.$$

But this rule is not a phrase structure rule since that permits only the rewriting of single symbols as other symbols and not such operations as permutation or deletion. A phrase structure rule shows us, so to speak, out of what lower constituents a higher constituent is composed, whereas the new rule shows us how whole strings of a certain kind can be transformed into strings of another kind — hence the name 'transformation rule'.

A transformational grammar will utilize rules of both sorts. So for example — and with qualifications — phrase structure rules would be used to derive the (a)-sentences above, while transformation rules will be used to derive the (b)-sentences from the (a)'s. One might expect, too, that since interrogatives, imperatives, or passives are systematically related to indicatives and actives, then the former will be transformationally derivable from the latter, these having been derived through phrase structure rules. In fact the picture is not so simple. Phrase structure rules will not be used to generate the active indicative *sentences,* but rather the strings which 'underlie' both them and the corresponding interrogatives, passives, etc. The active indicative sentence will, like the others, be transformationaly derived from this underlying string. However the underlying string will typically 'resemble' the active indicative sentence more than any of the others, since fewer steps of transformation will be required to arrive at it. Hence it is not too misleading to think of the other sentences as transformationally derived from simple active indicatives.

A transformational grammar, then, contains two kinds of rules: phrase structure ones for deriving certain strings, and transformation rules for deriving other strings, and eventually sentences, from these. The strings derived by phrase structure rules alone are the 'underlying' strings, and those derived from the cycle of transformations are the 'final derived' strings. The phrase marker for the underlying string is the 'underlying phrase marker', and that for the final derived string the 'final derived phrase marker'. The structure represented by the underlying phrase marker is the 'underlying' or 'deep' structure of the sentence, in contrast to the 'surface' or 'superficial' structure represented by the final derived phrase marker. For example, the final derived phrase marker for the sentence 'A wise man is honest' might be (roughly):

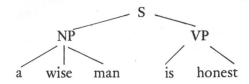

while the underlying phrase marker might be (roughly):

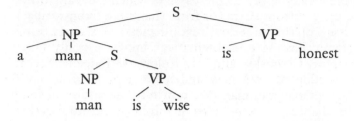

Transformation rules could then be described as those which map underlying onto surface phrase markers, or as those which relate deep to surface structures.

Why should a transformational grammar be preferred to a phrase structure grammar? It has been argued, by Postal for instance, that phrase structure rules are actually incapable of generating all well-formed sentences. But this is debatable. Most of the popular reasons are contained in this passage from Chomsky:

> A weaker, but perfectly sufficient demonstration of inadequacy would be to show that the theory (i.e. phrase structure grammar) can apply only clumsily; that is, to show that any grammar that can be constructed in terms of this theory will be extremely complex, *ad hoc,* and 'unrevealing' (1957 : p. 34).

It is relatively clear that a phrase structure grammar would be more complex, in the sense of having to employ more rules more often, than a transformational one. In a phrase structure grammar a separate rule for deriving each of the (b)-sentences would be needed, whereas a transformational grammar requires only the single rule for deriving them from the already derived (a)-sentences. The point about *ad hoc*ness is relatively clear too. There are various restrictions on what nouns can occur with what verbs in active sentences. In a phrase structure grammar these restrictions would have to be applied again, in an apparently *ad hoc* way, when separately deriving the corresponding passives. But in a transformational grammar, any restrictions imposed on the derivation of actives will automatically apply to the passives which are transformationally derived from them (or from their underlying strings).

The issue of the superior 'revealingness' of a transformational grammar is more problematical, but is certainly taken as crucial by Chomsky and his followers. Indeed, 'revealingness' is adopted as a new and major aim to be achieved by any acceptable grammar. (We return to the notion in some detail in chapter 5). One idea involved seems to be this: where sentences are definitely 'related', as are passives to their corresponding actives, the grammar must provide the means for displaying or picturing the relation. How better than to display the sentences as commonly derived from a single underlying string? The relation is then explained as the relation both sentences have to this single string. A phrase structure grammar, by having to provide quite separate phrase markers for the active and passive, would fail in this task.

A second idea is that only a transformational grammar can represent structural features in ways that accord with the 'intuitions' that native speakers have about sentences. To take the favourite example, consider the sentences 'John is easy to please' and 'John is eager to please'. The speaker knows, so it is said, that these differ markedly, in that 'John' is the object of the first sentence and the subject of the second. But there is no way of marking this difference in a phrase structure grammar which will provide identical phrase markers for the two sentences except for the occurrence of 'eager' rather than 'easy' in the final line. The difference is 'revealed', though, once we provide two very different underlying phrase markers, one clearly displaying 'John' as the object of the verb 'to please', the other displaying it as the subject. The apparent similarity between the sentences is a superficial one resulting from the ways the underlying strings have been transformed.

The third and most crucial idea is, as Chomsky puts it, that 'the surface structure generally gives us very little indication in itself of the meaning of the sentence' (1968 : p. 27). In other words, it is only by displaying underlying strings and structures that information essential to understanding what is meant by sentences is presented. For example, native speakers can quickly be brought to judge that the sentence 'The hunting of lions takes place at sunset' is ambiguous. Are the lions hunting or being hunted? A single surface phrase marker could not reveal this ambiguity. But it can be revealed, so it is said, by regarding the sentence as derivable from two very different underlying strings — one in which 'lions' is shown as the subject of 'to hunt', the other in which it is shown as the object. Sometimes, it is alleged, there is literally nothing in the actual sentence uttered, or the final derived string, corresponding to a constituent essential for grasping its meaning. Take the sentence 'Help the man!'. This is understood as meaning the same as 'You help the man!', not 'Everyone help the man!' or 'No one help the man!'. But this is not revealed by a surface phrase marker for the sentence, which will have as much in common with the markers for 'Everyone (no one) help the man!' as it will with the marker for 'You help the man!'. The solution is to provide an underlying phrase marker for 'Help the man!' which contains 'you' as a subject which is then deleted by a transformation rule from the final derived marker. We shall return to this kind of consideration, although it is precisely because of it, and the others already mentioned, that according to Katz,

> . . . a linguist must theoretically infer the existence of underlying phrase markers and why such phrase markers must have syntactic features that their corresponding final derived phrase markers lack (1966 : pp. 131-2)

A word should be said here about the other two components in a grammar, the semantic and phonological, which we have rather been ignoring. In fact, phonological theory will not concern us at all in this book, and only restricted aspects of the semantic theory, still underdeveloped, that Chomsky, borrowing from Fodor and Katz, harnessed with his syntactic theory. Still, a brief mention of the places these components occupy in the general picture of generative transformational theory is in order. It is, as we have been told, the underlying strings which contain the information essential to understanding what sentences mean, (transformations do not affect meaning). Hence the rules of the semantic component will operate upon the morphemes that replace grammatical formatives in deep structure. They will operate by permitting and restricting combinations of the conceptual elements in the meanings of these morphemes. The results of applying these rules will be 'semantic readings' of the sentences in question. (Some of the implications of this view of a semantic component are looked at in chapter 8). Phonological rules, on the other hand, will operate upon the morphemes of the final derived strings, since it is these which, so to speak, actually get uttered.

In brief, then: the grammatical theory that spawned the philosophical and psychological doctrines which interest us is one according to which the aims of a grammar are to generate all and only well-formed sentences of the language, together with structural descriptions of them, and semantic and phonological interpretations. Further, the grammar must be maximally 'revealing' of those aspects of sentences — ambiguity, synonymy, relatedness, etc. — which native speakers 'intuit' as belonging to them. These aims are achieved by a transformational grammar whose syntax generates underlying strings by phrase structure rules and final derived strings by transformation rules, and whose semantics operates upon underlying strings to derive semantic readings, and whose phonological component operates upon the final derived strings to derive phonetic interpretations.

'The principles of grammar form an important, and very curious, part of the philosophy of the human mind', wrote Sir James Beattie — and Chomsky concurs. But it may hardly be clear what contributions to philosophical psychology the theory of generative grammar can make. Is not it just a theory about strings of symbols and noises? In fact, though, we can already see that the theory as described is replete with psychological considerations. In setting as an aim of a grammar the generation of all and only well-formed sentences, we are already committed to a concern with men's judgments and beliefs. For unless these are consulted, we shall be unable to determine an initial selection of well- and ill-formed sentences. Certainly it will do no good simply observing what people say, for much of what they say, as the speakers are ready to agree, is not grammatical. In addition we saw that an important aim of a grammar, one which allegedly only a transformational grammar can achieve, was to reveal aspects of sentences so as to accord with speaker's 'intuitions'. So it is not just global judgments about well-formedness which will dictate the shape of a grammar, but also judgments about ambiguity, relations between sentences, synonymy, and so on.

But psychology, and philosophy too, really come into their own when we are told:

> The person who has acquired knowledge of a language has internalized a system of rules that relate sound and meaning in a particular way. The linguist constructing a grammar of a language is in effect proposing a hypothesis concerning this internalized system (Chomsky 1968 : p. 23).

So a grammar is not simply a linguist's construction, for the very rules, categories, structures, and principles he employs are, supposedly, part and parcel of every speaker's knowledge. Further, a grammar is essential in explaining human linguistic behaviour; for while this behaviour will depend upon many factors outside the linguist's frame of reference, it will depend in part upon the speaker's 'linguistic competence'. Now a grammar, according to Chomsky, is precisely a 'description of the ideal speaker-hearer's intrinsic competence. . . a reasonable model of language use will incorporate, as a basic component, the generative grammar that expresses the speaker-hearer's knowledge of the language' (1965 : p. 4 & p. 9). At one level, then, grammar may be a theory about the noises men make — but, in addition, so it is argued, a grammar is a description of men's knowledge and an essential element in explaining, *via* that knowledge, men's linguistic behaviour. This is a full-blown psychological doctrine whose peculiar status makes it, at the same time, a philosophical thesis.

But why are these claims made? Why should it be thought that a grammar is more than a linguist's device for talking about strings — that it is a crucial ingredient of every man's knowledge? For two broad and related reasons, I think. First, no other description of what it is to know a language

15

is, supposedly, adequate. In particular, the favourite alternative of treating knowledge of a language as a complex of dispositions to verbal behaviour is dismissed by Chomsky and others as vacuous. (See chapters 6 and 7). Second, speakers' knowledge of generative grammar must be invoked in order to explain certain crucial aspects of linguistic ability – in particular, the abilities to use language 'creatively' and to make appropriate 'intuitive' judgments about sentences. That is, a fluent speaker is able, in virtue of knowing his language, to produce and understand an indefinitely or infinitely large number of sentences. Such creativity, as it is called, could only be explained, it is argued, by supposing that speakers are following rules they have internalized, and not simply imitating or responding in a conditioned way. Further, the rules must be those of a transformational grammar, since many of the sentences the speaker can understand on the basis of ones he has learned only resemble the latter in deep structural respects. Hence 'inductive' rules, or 'analogies', which relate sentences only in superficial respects, could not explain his creative understanding. In addition to producing and understanding new sentences, the native speaker is able to make a vast number of judgments about them, expressing his 'linguistic intuitions'. Since the features he intuits are representable, so we have been told, only at the level of underlying structure, then it is only if we credit him with a grasp of a grammar incorporating such structures that we can explain his judgments. A grammar, we saw, had to 'reveal' features so as to accord with speakers' intuitions. Now we are told that if we are to explain how men are capable of these intuitions we must ascribe to them knowledge of the grammar in question.

It is not, of course, being suggested that the speaker-hearer's knowledge of a grammar is 'conscious', or that his acquaintance with its rules, categories, or structures is 'explicit'. On the contrary, it is stressed that the knowledge and acquaintance are 'tacit' and 'implicit'. According to Chomsky:

> Any interesting generative grammar will be dealing, for the most part, with mental processes that are far beyond the level of actual or even potential consciousness (1965 : p. 8).

These are heady claims and arguments, and ones which, for the moment, are at an uncomfortably high level of generality and abstraction. I won't yet try to sort them out, interpret them, or challenge them. But I do want to put the views that are emerging into a reasonably concise form so that we shall have a manageably short formulation to refer back to in what follows. I shall speak of the 'knowledge of language thesis' (KLT). KLT is the following thesis, or set of theses[10] :

> A person's knowledge of his language is constituted fundamentally by his 'internalization' of a generative transformational grammar for that language. The internalization itself takes the form of knowledge of the rules, categories, definitions, structures, etc. of the grammar — or, at any rate, the speaker has 'mentally represented' these to himself and is 'informed' about them. This knowledge, mental representation, or information is, typically, 'tacit' and 'unconscious', but nonetheless 'psychologically real'.[11] It is necessary to conceive of knowing a language in this way in order to explain, — *via* the speaker's following the rules of, and utilizing his information about, his grammar — the most significant aspects of linguistic behaviour; namely, creativity and the making of intuitive judgments.

While the various strands in KLT will be disentangled and examined later, a few clarificatory remarks are in order at this stage. First, what is psychologically and philosophically challenging in KLT does not depend upon accepting Chomsky's particular brand of generative transformational grammar. One could, for example, concede to the 'Generative Semanticists' their argument that there is no level of Chomskyan deep structure if that is defined as the level at which all lexical insertion can take place in a block prior to applying any 'toward the surface cyclic rules' (roughly, transformation rules).[12] But if the rival grammar were to employ rules and categories of comparable complexity, and to retain the notion of underlying structural levels of some sort — as Generative Semantics certainly does — then the hypothesis that such a grammar is internalized by speakers would be of the same interest as Chomsky's.

Second, I spoke of linguistic knowledge being 'fundamentally', not solely, constituted by knowledge of a grammar. Proponents of KLT could surely admit that various other items enter into a man's knowledge of his language — for example, 'conscious' and 'explicit' knowledge of the definitions of certain words. But I, like they, will relegate such items as being non-fundamental, for one could certainly imagine people who would be credited with knowing their language even though incapable of providing explicit definitions for the words they use.

Finally, if KLT is to be genuinely challenging, certain restrictions must be put upon what can be intended, by its proponents, by expressions like 'knowing a grammar' or 'following the rules of a grammar'. For no one would want to deny that speakers know and follow the rules of grammar if this is just a way of saying that they speak properly. If knowing a grammar, and hence a language, is simply know *how* — being able to form and understand sentences — then of course every native speaker knows the grammar of his language. Clearly proponents of KLT do not intend to say simply this. Knowing a language, insists Chomsky, is not 'merely a matter of 'knowing how' ' (1968 : p. 22). Indeed, they *must* mean more than this, else some of the claims they make about knowledge of grammar become nonsensical. Remember, first, that knowledge of a grammar is supposed to explain verbal behaviour, which it could hardly do if equated with it. Second, the knowledge was said to be 'tacit' and 'unconscious' — but it would make no sense, or a quite unintended sense, to speak of tacit or unconscious fluent verbal behaviour. (Or of explicit and conscious behaviour either). Third it was stressed that the rules, categories, etc. of the grammar have 'psychological reality', that they are 'mentally represented' by speakers. I take it such terms are used precisely in order to draw a contrast between the real nature of knowledge of grammar and mere know *how*. So when, in future, I speak of 'non-trivial' knowledge of grammar, of its rules, structures, categories, and so on, I mean the kind postulated by KLT; the kind which would make at least initial sense of the above claims; and the kind which not all of us would automatically concede.

I assume that KLT, taken at face value (which is how I shall take it), *is* startling and challenging. It is surely startling to be told that all fluent speakers, however obtuse and dull otherwise, have mastered, internalized, and come to know enormously complex rules, highly abstract categories, and structures of sufficient obscurity to divide professional linguists as to their proper description. It is even more startling to be told that these remarkable feats have been performed by children as young as three years. Put crudely, these little children know as much as Professors Chomsky, Lakoff, or Fillmore about their grammar — it's just that they cannot formulate, and are not aware of, what it is they know. (If somebody says I am parodying KLT, the reply is that these startling implications should certainly be drawn from it if we are to take seriously the talk of speakers 'knowing' and 'mastering' the rules of a grammar. If he does not like the implications, he should give up these ways of talking; in other words, give up KLT). And KLT is certainly challenging to whole styles of thought in psychology and philosophy. If knowledge of a language consists in knowing a generative grammar, then it can not be the result of any learning strategies proposed by traditional psychology. If it is the internalization of such a grammar which explains linguistic behaviour, then the behaviour is not explicable in terms of anything like 20th century S-R psychology. And, as the reader can judge and as we shall elaborate, if the conception of knowledge involved is correct then what Wittgenstein, Ryle, and Quine, to take just three philosophers, have said about knowledge is simply wrong.

My penultimate remarks in this chapter take us back to where we began — with innateness. I want to look at the connection between the new innateness hypothesis and the wider set of doctrines comprising KLT. Suppose we accept KLT. The question would then arise as to how speakers have acquired their knowledge of the rules, categories, or structures of their grammars. It might be suggested that these are abstracted from the features and regularities of the speech children observe about them. But this answer, reminiscent of traditional empiricist accounts of the genesis of general ideas, is forcefully rejected by Chomsky and his followers.

> . . .knowledge of language cannot arise by application of step-by-step inductive operations (segmentation, classification, substitution procedures, 'analogy', association, conditioning, and so on) of any sort that have been developed or discussed within linguistics, psychology, or philosophy (1967 : p. 11).

But why? Well, we have already encountered the assertion that a person's understanding of a new sentence on the basis of ones he has learned in the past will often depend upon deep structural relations between it and them, and not upon the surface relations which are a poor guide to semantic similarity. Hence the rules he is utilizing concern aspects of deep structure. But deep structural features are, typically, 'remote from the physical signal' (Chomsky 1968 : p. 53). That is, they may have little 'resemblance' to features in the final derived string which are the ones, as it were, which provide the materials for the sentence as actually spoken. It may even be, as we were told in connection with the example of 'Help the man!', that nothing in the spoken sentence expresses a certain deep grammatical element.

The next step is to argue that the only 'observable' features of a sentence are those which are highly 'correlated' with the actual spoken sounds, in which case deep features, which are 'remote from the physical signal', are not 'observable'. Subjects, for example, will not be 'observable' since, as we saw in connection with our friend John, there is little or no correlation between an expression's place in the spoken sentence and its role as the subject of the sentence. But in that case, any empiricist model of the acquisition of grammar, in terms of abstraction, inductive generalization, association, analogy, or whatever, is doomed. For it is essential to any such account that the abstractions, inductions, etc. should be performed upon observable features of the data concerned. Since, on the contrary, the rules and structures arrived at by speakers concern and refer to 'unobservable' elements they cannot have been internalized through any set of procedures deserving the title 'empiricist'.

To arrive at the rules and structures, so the alternative suggestion goes, the child must be originally acquainted with both the general categories of grammar and with at least the formal aspects of its rules. In other words, both 'substantive' and 'formal' universals must be part of the child's innate intellectual equipment.[13] Given this equipment he is able, in terms of its ingredients, to hypothesize as to the nature of the rules and structures of the grammar of his own particular language. Some of the hypotheses he will reject in the face of the data he encounters, the utterances he hears about him (though these might be compatible with the data of some other language), or on grounds of simplicity and the like. Finally, he will be left with just those hypotheses which do suitably conform with the data, and these will constitute his grammar. So while experience certainly plays a role in the acquisition of language, it does so only by providing tests for the hypotheses formulated in terms of pre-experiential categories and forms.

> Experience serves not to provide the things to be copied by the mind, as in the empiricist's account, but to help eliminate false hypotheses about the rules of a language (Katz 1966 : p. 278 n.).

It is worth noting, I think, that if this style of argument is correct then the frequent appeals made by the new innatists to the speed with which children learn language, or to the 'degenerate' nature of their linguistic environments, are superfluous in establishing the innateness hypothesis. It is the nature of the knowledge acquired, not its speed or manner of acquisition, which demands an explanation in terms of innateness. Analogously, Descartes' rejection of empiricist accounts of how the idea of substance is acquired in no way depended upon the speed with which it was acquired or upon people's lack of acquaintance with lumps of wax or whatever. If no one picked up the idea of substance until they were octogenarians accustomed to finding twenty lumps of wax a day this would not alter the force of Descartes' argument.

21

No doubt the above argument for innateness is a hot-potch of confusion. But, for the moment, I am concerned only to trace the connection of the doctrine with the more general doctrines of KLT. As I said earlier, I shall spend relatively little time on direct discussion of innateness, though I hope there will be no doubt as to the bearing on this issue of our more general discussions. Is knowing a language what KLT says it is? If not, what is it? These are the main questions discussed.

My final remarks in this chapter concern its title. Why do I refer to Chomsky and proponents of KLT as the 'new rationalists'? Partly because they refer to themselves as rationalists. But why do they do this? Needless to say, not a great deal turns upon whether the epithet is applied or not. 'Rationalist', like its twin 'empiricist', has become too versatile for much weight to be placed on it. But I think there is some value in applying the epithet, and reflection upon why this is will provide us with an excuse for stressing various wider aspects of, and contrasts with, KLT.

One reason for talking of a new rationalism, of course, is the new innateness hypothesis recently sketched. Yet there is a good sense in which a doctrine of innateness is at most a corollary, however important, rather than a basic platform of rationalism, old or new. The 17th century rationalists did not begin by postulating innate knowledge and then search around for items to fill the bill. Rather, they sought to demonstrate the existence of knowledge of a certain kind which, it then seemed to them, must be regarded as innate. And they were rationalists in virtue of the kind of knowledge they tried to demonstrate, not the corollary that such knowledge must be innate. It is not the hypothesizing of innate ideas or knowledge of just any old kind that makes one a rationalist. Were the only principles known innately like Sir Matthew Hale's 'The obscene parts and actions are not to be exposed to the publick view', there would be nothing rationalistic about innatism. What is characteristic of rationalism are the claims that ideas or items of knowledge are present to the mind by virtue, so to speak, of the mind's own activities, and that further they are appreciated 'by that part of the mind distinguished as the reason or understanding' (Edgley : p. 12). There is nothing rationalistic, for example, in the notion of an innate moral sense which, without any aid from normal sense experience, informs us of intuitable ethical properties. For grasping the idea of 'passively' intuited properties would require neither 'active' mental powers nor exercise of rationality. We are on the way to rationalism with Descartes' claim that our ideas even of colours must be innate, since they 'have no likeness' to what can 'reach our mind. . .through our organs of sense' (p. 443) — so that they are not 'passively' received copies of external properties. And we have arrived at rationalism with Descartes' account of our knowledge of God — an idea which has no resemblance to anything provided by the senses, and one, moreover, that belongs to us in virtue of our powers of reason and understanding, and not, like the ideas of sirens or hippogryphs, in virtue of our imaginative and fictive powers.

No doubt this talk of the mind's 'activity' and of its 'powers of reason and understanding' is obscure enough. But my interest is only in finding echoes of such talk among the new rationalists; echoes which will merit them that title. And these are not hard to find. Our 'ideas' of deep structural features are precisely those which, lacking 'resemblance' or 'correlation' with the data of the senses (noises and final derived strings), are forged within the mind and not, as Katz puts it, 'copied by' it.[14] Further the mind is as 'active' in this direction as one could wish. It *constructs* hypotheses, *interprets* data in terms of them, and *tests* them against data. Such mental activities are, moreover, supremely ones of reason. A grammar of a language is a vast axiomatic system. A speaker who judges a sentence to be well-formed, or to have a certain meaning, is doing nothing less than deducing information from the system of rules he has internalized. These echoes are, perhaps, no clearer than what they echo — but they are echoes nonetheless.

The mind, so the rationalist argues, plays a crucial, large, and active role in the acquisition of ideas — more crucial, larger, and more active at any rate, than the empiricist allows. But a different sense can be given to 'the mind's crucial role', from which a different doctrine results; a doctrine, which by a transference of the term, also gets called 'rationalist'. I have in mind what is popularly referred to today as 'mentalism'; what, at other times, has been called 'intellectualism', 'cognitivism', and in derogatory mood 'the doctrine of the ghost in the machine'. The mind plays a crucial role in the sense that reference to its activities, processes, structures, or whatever, figures essentially in explanations of intelligent behaviour. Mentalism, and hence rationalism so construed, is to be contrasted with all the myriad forms of behaviourism.[15] Now KLT, of course, is avowedly, indeed agressively, mentalistic.

> . . . linguistic theory is mentalistic, since it is concerned with discovering a mental reality underlying actual behavour (Chomsky 1965 : p. 4).

Now is not the moment to detail the dispute between mentalists and their rivals. Suffice it to say that we find mentalism in action when Chomsky explains a person's ability to recognize that 'In has lived Mary Princeton' is not a proper interrogative form by his 'knowing that' a certain structure-dependent operation has not been performed in deriving it (1968 : p. 52); when Fodor and Bever explain a person's subjective perception of the position of clicks made during utterances in terms of the 'psychological reality' of his acquaintance with syntactic structure; or when McNeill (1970) explains the child's saying 'teached' and 'eated' in terms of overextending a rule for inflection that he has internalized. And suffice it to say that we find mentalism criticized in Ryle's dismissal of the 'intellectualist legend' according to which each bit of intelligent rule-governed behaviour must be preceded by an act of consulting a rule that the agent has represented to himself; in Wittgenstein's rejection of the idea that classifying new instances proceeds by comparing them with prototype images in the head; or in Quine's view that linguistic competence is no more than a set of dispositions to verbal behaviour. We might generalize to the extent of saying that one veers towards or away from mentalism in so far as one is generous or parsimonious in postulating mental activities or processes in explanations of behaviour. KLT is very generous, hence mentalistic, and hence in the derived sense, rationalistic.[16]

So much for preliminaries, some of which have been unavoidably vague. I hope they have not been so vague as to have provided no idea of what it is that will concern us in this book.

Notes to Chapter 1

1   In the following passage for example:
> . . . why should it (the soul) not always think, when it is a thinking substance? Why is it strange that we do not remember the thoughts it has had in the womb or in a stupor, when we do not even remember most of those we have had when grown up in good health, and awake? (vol. II : p. 210).

2   Chomsky himself says there is no 'a priori' reason why languages should, as they all do, employ 'structure-dependent' operations (1968 : p. 52).

3   Lyons, for example, writes:
> It is upon this kind of similarity between languages . . . that he (Chomsky) rests his case for a rationalist philosophy of language (p. 103).

But this does not accurately reflect Chomsky's own assessment of the significance of universals which, he says, merely *'lead one to suspect'* an innate component (1967 : p. 4 My italics).

4   See, for instance, H. Hiz.

5   Hume, I think, is expressing this attitude when he writes:
> If innate be equivalent to natural, then all perceptions and ideas of the mind must be allowed to be innate or natural, in whatever sense we take the latter word (p. 23).

6   See P. Unger. It would miss the point, incidentally, to say that our monster's knowledge is not innate since the people from whom it is constructed had experiences. It is not essential to the example that the monster is created from other human beings; we could just as well suppose it to be made of metal. It is its behaviour, not its manner of construction that is important.

7   More detailed introductions can be found in Lyons, Cooper (1973a), and Katz (1966). Tougher going, but essential for a full understanding of the theory is Chomsky (1965).

8   As a matter of history, Chomsky gives the syntactic component far more work to do in his later writings (e.g. 1965) than in his original ones (e.g. 1957).

9   Chomsky has denied that the issue is anything more than term-
      inological (1971).
10   This thesis is argued for, defended, or simply assumed in the
      following writings among many others: Chomsky (1965, 1967,
      1968, 1969a, 1970), Katz (1966, 1972), Fodor (1966, 1968a),
      Slobin, McNeill (1966, 1970), and with reservations Vendler.
11   All these terms can be found used in Katz (1967) and Fodor
      (1968a)
12   See G. Lakoff.
13   For explanation of these terms, see Chomsky (1965).
14   Actually, the sense in which ideas lacked resemblance with data of
      the senses for Descartes is very different from the sense in which
      deep structures lack resemblance with sentences for Chomsky. See
      Cooper (1972).
15   It is interesting to note here that Vendler's recent book, which
      is basically a critique of behaviourist accounts of thinking, is
      sub-titled 'An essay in rationalist psychology'.
16   It needs to be stressed that the mentalism in question is not
      an ontological thesis, like dualism, to the effect that mind
      is a distinct kind of substance. Chomsky and Katz are quite
      happy to accept the possibility that the mental activities and
      processes essential to explaining behaviour will one day be identi-
      fied with physiological or neurological ones. See especially Katz
      (1967).

Chapter 2

Competence and Performance

This chapter ought not to have been necessary. That it is, is due partly to the obligation all writers in this field seem to feel for mentioning the competence/performance distinction, however overblown its importance. But it is necessary, too, because the assumptions I want to challenge in it, however unwarranted, are made only too often. Uncritical students, misled by uncritical psycholinguists, seem to swallow them without a sign of queasiness.

My modest aim in this chapter is to show that KLT does need to be argued for and that it cannot be instantly established on the basis of some allegedly obvious assumptions or definitions. Yet this is just what some writers seem to be doing, and if their assumptions and definitions are accepted, the need for further argument in support of KLT is obviated. The *locus classicus* in this connection is p. 4 of Chomsky's *Aspects of the Theory of Syntax.* He writes:

> We thus make a fundamental distinction between *competence* (the speaker-hearer's knowledge of his language) and *performance* (the actual use of language in concrete situations).

A few lines later, competence is identified with the 'mastery' of 'the underlying system of rules that . . . he (the speaker-hearer) puts to use in actual performance'. We are offered, therefore, two equations, both of which seem to be thought of as obvious:

Competence = Knowledge of a language
Competence = Mastery of an underlying system of rules

It follows that a person's knowledge of a language is his mastery of a system of rules. Katz, even more briefly, defines 'linguistic competence' as 'the internalized rules that he (the speaker-hearer) knows' (1972: p. 51)[1]. Add to this the view that the knowledge in question is of a non-trivial kind which has 'mental reality', together with the claim that the rules are those of a generative transformational grammar, and you have arrived at KLT. It then seems that all we need to establish KLT is the assumption that there is such a thing as linguistic competence distinguishable from linguistic performance.

I will return to these equations after a glance at the general notion of competence. The distinction between competence and performance in language is sometimes thought to be the same as, or similar to, de Saussure's between 'langue' and 'parole'. But this is not so. His distinction was between one's stock of linguistic materials and the utterances that could be composed out of them. To suppose that this is similar to the distinction between competence and performance is like treating the distinction between dough and loaves as similar to that between the ability to bake and baking.

Some writers, peculiarly, have doubted if there is a genuine distinction between competence and performance. But of course there is. One can and must distinguish between the ability to do something and actually doing something. The conceptual distinction is there even when a person does everything he can. As Shaw remarked, teachers excepted, those who can do. Precisely because the distinction has to be made, in whatever area of behaviour one takes, it sounds initially unpromising that anything momentous could hang upon it when drawn in the area of linguistic behaviour. The realization that it needs to be drawn here, as elsewhere, would not seem a startling or profound one. It could be pointed out, no doubt, that in this field people's abilities far outrun their actual performances. Given the 'creativity' of speakers mentioned on p. 16, then clearly no speaker will ever perform those linguistic deeds that he is, in some sense, capable of. But this scarcely distinguishes linguistic behaviour. No golfer, however talented and energetic, will perform all those golfing feats of which he is, in some sense, capable.

Perhaps I will be told I am missing the point; that while the distinction is obvious enough, it has peculiar importance in language since the competence in question must be identified with knowledge of a system of rules — and *that* surely is significant. No doubt it is significant. The trouble is that it is just this identification which needs to be examined. Certainly I cannot doubt the need for a distinction between competence and performance, but I can doubt that this is co-extensive with any distinction between knowledge and its application, or between mastery of a system of rules and actual employment of it. In fact I can do more than doubt this. I can show that any claim to their co-extensiveness must be mistaken.

Whatever competence might exactly be, it is a type of ability. A sensitive classification would, no doubt, distinguish many kinds of ability — competence, capacity, capability, potential, and so on. For our purposes it is enough to realize that talking about a person's competence is talking about what he *can* do. Now to say that a person can do something is to say something conditional in form. It is, roughly, to say what he would do if certain conditions held. (It may be that not all 'can's' are, as Austin put it, 'constitutionally iffy' in this way. These would be the 'can's at issue in debates about free action. Perhaps it has to be true of a person that he could have acted otherwise even under the self same conditions, (including his history), if we are to say he acted freely. But the 'can's that concern us are not these. The ability referred to by 'linguistic competence' is not the ability to have said something different from what was said under just the condition, including historical ones, which obtained).

It is clear that the truth or falsity of 'He can do X' may vary according to what conditionals are intended. For example, 'He can win a golf championship' might be intended to convey any of the following:

> If he concentrates on his shots, he will win.
> If he practices for a few weeks, he will win.
> If he learns golf, he will one day win a championship, so great is his talent for ball games.
> If he has a brain operation and is fitted with some artificial

limbs, I guarantee — so great is my faith in modern medicine — that he will one day win a golf championship.

All, some, or none of these might be true of a given individual. Equally the claim that a person is able to understand an utterance might be intended as any, or many more, of the the following:

If he is not distracted, he will understand it.
If he brushes up on his French, he will understand it.
If he learns French, he will be able to understand this and many other sentences.
If he has a brain operation at our hospital, he will be able to understand even that sentence.

Once again, all, some, or none of these might be true of a given individual.

It follows that if any substance is to be given to the claim that a person is competent to do something, a range of conditionals must be specified or presupposed. To say that a person is able to understand and produce sentences he never does understand or produce will, if there is any substance in it, be to say that these specified conditionals are true of him. And it is importance to realize that other conditionals will not be true of him so that, in any number of ways, he is not able to understand or produce these sentences. John may be able to understand 'Je suis heureux' in the sense that he will understand it if he learns French and listens closely, but not be able to understand it by simply listening closely. This rather elementary point should cut through the sterile debate as to whether a person can 'really' understand sentences two hundred words long, or sentences with a dozen or so embedded relative clauses. In some senses he can, in others he can not.

What range of conditionals do linguists typically have in mind when talking of linguistic competence — and why? The protases of the conditionals usually include at least the following:

If he did not suffer from limitations of memory . . .
If he was not subject to lapses of attention . . .
If he was not subject to emotional excitement, outside interferences . . .

The blanks are filled in by descriptions of the person's understanding or production of sentences, or of his making judgments about sentences, such as that they are ambiguous, ungrammatical, or whatever. It is conditionals like these, and not ones like

If he had learned English . . .
If he was not a new-born baby . . .
If he did not suffer from a totally deprived linguistic environment . . .
If he was cured of his brain tumour . . .

in terms of which competence is identified. Persons of whom these latter conditionals were true would be able, in certain senses, to understand sentences they never will understand, but they are not linguistically competent in the relevant sense. Very roughly, then, linguistic competence is what would be reflected in performance were it not for limitations on memory, time, attention, emotional detachment, and the like.

But why is competence understood in terms of these conditionals and not others? One answer which would not do is: because these conditionals state the conditions under which a person's purely linguistic knowledge, or mastery of purely linguistic rules, would be reflected in performance. One thing that is objectionable in this answer is that it presupposes just the thesis, KLT, which is in question. But apart from that, and even if we were to grant KLT, the answer would be unacceptable by virtue of its circularity. For the only reply there could be to the question 'What is purely linguistic knowledge?' would be 'That knowledge which is reflected in performance *under certain conditions*'. But in that case, the suggested answer presupposes some way of identifying the relevant conditions under which people who are competent will understand sentences, and cannot be used to determine what these are. It is not just linguistic competence, but 'purely linguistic knowledge', that will be delineated by specification of the relevant conditionals. We shall see, too, that the suggested answer implies there is a straightforwardly *correct* answer to the question, whereas what is needed is a decision that is, to some degree, arbitrary.

A more promising rationale of the linguist's notion of competence would proceed along different lines. There are some limitations which affect all human performance — those on memory and powers of concentration, for example. There are others which affect only certain kinds of performance. Having no eye for the ball will interfere with one's batting and catching, but not one's chess or wine-tasting. There may even be some which affect only one kind of performance. Now if we are concerned to assess a person's prowess at some particular activity, our interest will not be in limitations of the first sort. That Jack Nicklaus' driving would deteriorate after the 800th hole shows he is a normal human being and nothing especially about his golf. Equally the fact that a man will lose track of my meaning after the fifth or sixth relative clause shows he is of normal human intelligence and nothing about his linguistic abilities in particular. Ideally we would want a list of limitations which affect linguistic performance and no other kind, so that we could say a person is linguistically competent unless he suffers from these. But there are few, if any, limitations which will affect linguistic performance alone. The linguist will therefore select from a long list of factors affecting performance, both linguistic and non-linguistic, those which are *relatively* specific to language skills. A disability for forming questions will, whereas general limitations on attention, will not figure on the selected list. The person who is linguistically incompetent will then be the one who suffers from these limitations.

However it is not that simple. Having selected an initial list of factors relevant to linguistic competence, the linguist will then use this list to dictate selection of further factors according to their similarities or analogies with the original ones. Thus a limitation, like stuttering, may be relatively specific to language behaviour but, because of its lack of analogy with other selected factors, not figure in a description of competence. By employing this approach the linguist can hope to arrive at a reasonably homogenous set of limitations on competence.

It is important to realize that often it is a matter of choice, to a degree arbitrary but influenced by a variety of considerations including those of simplicity, homogeneity, and cohesion with general grammatical theory, what factors limit competence. Consider, for example, the person who is poor at grasping metaphors, in particular those employed in aesthetic descriptions. Is he linguistically incompetent or is he, rather, suffering from some lack of sensibility that affects, *inter alia,* his verbal understanding? Our decision here will be influenced, no doubt, by how we conceive of metaphor within linguistic theory. If, like Cohen and Margalit, we think of metaphorical uses as generated in an orderly, rule-governed way from literal uses, then we might treat failure to grasp metaphors as analogous to failing to understand grammatical transformations, and hence as a reflection on linguistic competence. If, like Goodman (1968), we stress that aesthetic metaphors are simply *seen*, without rule-governed connection with literal uses, we might prefer the other option. But these considerations are only influences and would by no means finally determine what we have to say. In other cases we might appeal to general psychological theory to motivate our decisions. For instance, to the extent that aphasia is considered as a sensory-motor disorder, unconnected with a general difficulty in formulating symbols, we shall prefer not to treat it as a form of linguistic incompetence.

There is another way in which a linguist's notion of competence will involve selection and a degree of arbitrariness. Competence is what is reflected in performance under certain conditions. But what is linguistic performance? Or, rather, what range of performances are we interested in? One person may talk rudely, another politely. Is this difference in performance one that a theory of competence should take account of? It is fairly clear that Chomsky, for one, severely limits the kind of performance for which a theory of competence is meant to account. Roughly speaking, he is not concerned with the 'pragmatic' dimension of speech, with whether or not a person's utterances are 'appropriate to the context in which they are made' (Campbell and Wales 1970: p. 247). A speaker, for Chomsky, can be perfectly competent even though all his utterances are ones we should dismiss as out of place, silly, and so on. I mention this, not in order to criticize, but to stress how a linguist's notion of competence is bound to have resulted from his selective preferences. 'Linguistic competence' does not describe some readily identifiable and discrete human ability, but a variety of abilities that linguists, for purposes of their own, find it convenient to group together.

These comments over the last few pages, on the selection of conditionals in terms of which to specify linguistic competence, have been somewhat of a digression away from my direct critical concern, though they have been, I hope, pertinent to a wider issue of some interest. My main concern was to block a particular, over-facile route to KLT *via* a series of definitions or equations concerning competence, knowledge, and mastery of rules. To block this route, all we need do is to bear in mind that statements about ability, and so about linguistic competence, *are* conditional in form. Given this, it is surely a categorical error to equate linguistic competence with (non-trivial) knowledge. To say that a person is competent to do something is to say he would do it if certain conditions held. To say that he (non-trivially) knows something is to say nothing similarly conditional in form. Linguistic competence can no more *be* knowledge than the ability to win the golf championship can be knowing that it starts at 11 a.m., that a 'wood' is needed for the tee-shot, and so on.

Actually we have seen there is no need to deny a sense of 'know' in which statements about a person's knowledge would be conditional statements about what he would do if . . . Perhaps 'He knows how to ride a bicycle' does mean, roughly, that if he is put on a bicycle then, *ceteris paribus,* he will ride off on it. And even if this is not a proper sense of 'know' we could invent it. In such a sense, naturally, competence could be equated with knowledge. But, as we have also seen, this cannot be the kind of knowledge that Chomsky and proponents of KLT intend. For there were a number of things they wanted to say about knowledge which could not be said about the knowledge just mentioned, the knowledge I earlier called 'trivial'. Trivial knowledge, the mere ability to do something, cannot be unconscious (or conscious) — though, which is quite different, one can be unaware that one has it.[2] Nor can trivial knowledge explain one's performances, not at any rate in the sense of giving causes or reasons for them. 'He produces sentences because he is able to' is not an explanation, or not an explanation of the sort that the notion of competence is meant to provide.

Analogous considerations apply when equating competence with mastery of a system of rules. Competence can no more *be* that, than the ability to win the golf championship can be knowing the rules in the club manual. Again, we may find or invent a sense of 'mastery of rules' in which to say that a person has mastered the rules is to say no more than that he is able to do certain things under certain conditions. But, once more, this cannot be a sense to suit proponents of KLT. Such mastery cannot be unconscious (or conscious) in a relevant sense (see note 2), nor could it explain performance in the intended manner.

There is a fairly predictable reply to which I have been saying. It might run:

Granted it is a mistake to equate linguistic competence with (non-trivial) knowledge. Still, the point is easily amended.

It is knowledge which underlies competence. A person is competent by virtue of such knowledge. The same amendment can be made in connection with mastery of rules. Competence is not mastery, but it does result from it.

So what, clarity apart, have I achieved, given that my point can be met by a fairly simple amendment? Well, I did not set out to achieve very much in this chapter: merely to disabuse the uncritical of a particularly simple-minded adoption of KLT. But I do think that a little more than clarity and disabuse of the uncritical has been gained.

In the first place the flavour of self-evidence that KLT seems to have for so many people is diluted once the above amendment is forced. If competence is simply equated with knowledge and mastery of rules then, it appears, all we need do to establish KLT is to accept that there is such a thing as linguistic competence — and who wants to deny that? But once it is seen that knowledge and mastery of the relevant sort are to be brought in, if at all, by way of explaining the abilities involved in linguistic competence, the question is left wide open as to whether there is such knowledge or mastery. We can admit the need to talk of linguistic competence without, *ipso facto,* admitting such knowledge or mastery. Whether or not competence is explained by, or results from, the relevant knowledge and mastery will be a matter of controversy: the claim that it is will need to be supported by argument. There might be other ways of explaining competence, or perhaps no explanation is required at all. Certainly, in any number of areas, reference to a person's knowledge will figure in explanation of how he comes to have a certain ability. I can, and you can not, do well on the history test because I do, and you do not, know the dates of the Kings of England. But equally, in any number of areas, appeal to a person's knowledge may not be required in explanation of a person's abilities. The difference between the man who can fill his pipe successfully and the man who strews tobacco all over the floor need not be that the first knows something the second does not. Maybe he is more practised, or maybe he has the more nimble fingers and thumbs. So whether or not an ability results from knowledge of some kind will always bear examination in every case.

No one would deny, of course, that most speakers have some non-trivial knowledge of language, of a quite untroversial sort, and that it is sometimes necessary to refer to such knowledge in explaining certain performances. A speaker may know, for example, the definition of 'bachelor', or that 'John is smiling' is an acceptable sentence. But existence of knowledge of this kind provides no sort of support for KLT. For, as Harman notes, such knowledge

> . . is not the knowledge of particular rules of a transformational grammar. It is, as it were, knowledge about the output of such a grammar (1967 : p. 81).

Or we may put it like this: knowledge of this sort is expressed by those who have it in the form of judgments, and these judgments are *performances.* They are performances of just the kind that the knowledge postulated by KLT is supposed to account for.[3] So the knowledge avowed by such judgments is not the type at issue. Unfortunately it is only too easy to slip from the uncontroversial claim that a speaker knows a sentence to be ambiguous, or grammatically acceptable, or whatever, to the claim that he knows the rules, structures, etc. of a transformational grammar. For if an ambiguous sentence *is* one derived from two underlying structures, must not the person who knows it to be ambiguous know it to be derived from two underlying structures? Clearly, though, there is something questionable about this inference. Indeed, any inference of the form 'A knows that X', 'X = Y', therefore 'A knows that Y' is questionable' (We return to this in chapter 5)

In the second place, something happens to the logic of the argument for KLT once we cease to equate competence with both knowledge and mastery of a system of rules. From the two equations

Competence = Knowledge of a language

and

Competence = Mastery of a system of rules

one can derive, obviously, the equation

Knowledge of a language = Mastery of a system of rules.

And it is this equation, with appropriate interpretations of the terms, which yields KLT. But no such equation is warranted by the amended claims

Knowledge of a language must be postulated to explain linguistic competence

and

Mastery of a system of rules must be postulated to explain linguistic competence.

For we might now grant that while there is knowledge of language, in some sense, explanatory of competence, and while there is mastery of rules, in some sense, which is also explanatory, the two explanatory factors are by no means identical. The knowledge in question need not be of a system of rules, nor the mastery of rules in question be in the form of knowledge. Knowledge may enter into some explanations, mastery of rules into others. For example, one might explain the difference in two men's abilities to understand the speech of Yorkeshiremen by pointing out that the one does, and the other does not, know that Yorkshiremen typically leave out articles before nouns. This knowledge has nothing to do with mastery of rules. Conversely, we might grant that a fluent speaker has, in some sense or another, mastered some principle of transformational grammar, but in the absence of further argument, there will be no reason to treat this mastery as a piece of knowledge, or as something which is 'mentally represented', or as expressing what the speaker is 'informed about'.

The upshot, then, is that each platform of KLT requires argument and justification. Therefore let us proceed to the weightier problem of whether these can in fact be given.

Notes to Chapter 2

1   Another example of this definitional route to KLT is found in Slobin. On p. 6 he writes:
> The sort of competence in which we are interested can be defined, in part, (as) . . . the language-user's knowledge of grammaticality, grammatical relations, sentence relations, ambiguity, and so on.

And on p. 19:
> The sort of linguistic competence referred to here is a system of rules which relates semantic interpretations of sentences of their acoustic phonetic representations.

2   If by 'unconscious knowledge of language' were meant 'unawareness of one's ability to produce and understand sentences', there could be very few speakers whose knowledge of their language is unconscious, since few can be unaware that they have the above abilities. Since Chomsky insists that the knowledge speakers have of language is unconscious, this cannot be what he wants to mean by 'unconscious knowledge of language'.

3   See Slobin, for example: '. . . we are dealing with a very limited sort of performance here, such as rating sentences for grammaticality' (p. 7).

Chapter 3

Rules and Rule-Following

According to KLT there are rules of language, as portrayed in generative grammars, which speakers tacitly know or, in some unconscious way, 'mentally represent'. For example, there are transformation rules relating deep and surface structures that they know. So one thing that has to be established is that there are rules of language, and not simply statistical regularities in speech. But is also has to be established that speakers in some sense follow these rules; that, in the favoured terminology, they have 'internalized' or 'mastered' them. It is not generally the case that knowing rules necessitates following them. I know the rules of Russian roulette but, with any luck, I shall never follow them. In the case of linguistic behaviour, though, the prime reason for saying that speakers know the rules is that they follow them. So unless it can be shown that speakers follow the rules of generative grammar, there will be little enough reason for supposing they know them. The question of knowledge I defer until the next chapter. The immediate concern is with rules and rule-following.

It must be shown, then, that speakers are rule-followers, where rule-following is contrasted with mere accordance or conformity with rules. The famous monkey who will eventually type the works of Shakespeare will be producing sentences which accord with rules of English; but we should not want to describe him as following the rules, as being guided by them, as regulating his behaviour by them, or as having mastered them. It will not be enough, however, to show that speakers follow rules in some sense or another. It must be the right sense; one which will allow the claims of KLT to be intelligible. For example, the rule-following must be of a kind that could *explain* linguistic performance. What I shall try to argue in this chapter is that, while we may speak of people following the rules of language, they do not do so in a sense which permits conclusions central to KLT to be drawn.

Are there rules of language, though? It has been argued that there are not, on both weak and more respectable grounds. But — in a dull enough sense to be sure — there certainly are. For there are certainly standards of correct and incorrect speech. In other words, there are regularities from which deviations are not merely unusual but variously criticizable. Utterances so deviating can be ungrammatical, or meaningless, or garbled. They are ones which ought not to be produced. Hence the statements describing these regularities can also be treated as statements of rules. For example, speakers usually follow transitive verbs with noun phrases. If someone doesn't then, generally, he will be speaking ungrammatically. So 'V_{tr} is followed by NP' can be taken as a statement of a rule. (Actually, not all rules will be like this one. Not all of them *need* be employed for speech to be grammatical; rather they are 'permissive' rules which, if employed, retain grammaticality. You do not have to say 'I looked the number up' instead of 'I looked up the number'. So the rule

$$NP + v + part. + NP \rightarrow NP + v + NP + part.$$

is permissive, (unless the second NP is a pronoun)).

While there surely are rules, we are not absolved from utmost care in our talk of rules and regularities. Unless we are careful we shall likely exaggerate the extent to which language is rule-governed. First, it is by no means easy to establish what the regularities are. Since much speech is ungrammatical, the relevant regularities cannot be simply extracted from a corpus of observed speech. Rather they must be extracted from an 'idealized' corpus of the speech which would be produced under especially favoured conditions — where, for instance, there are no distractions. This means linguists must rely upon people's judgments about what would be said under such conditions. Unfortunately people's judgments may be uncertain and mutually conflicting. So, over a wide range, we shall not be able to say if there is a regularity which can serve as a rule. We might allow our grammar to decide for us in such cases, but a decision is what it is.

Second, there is a danger that we shall impose rather than discover regularities, and so invent rather than discover rules. The danger is particularly present when dealing with children's speech, where the technique of asking for speakers' judgments about grammaticality or meaningfulness is unfruitful. It is a trap, I fear, that too many developmental psycholinguists have fallen into. For example, a young child may say, with apparent indifference, either 'That is my book' or 'That my book'. There would seem, therefore, no great regularity in children's use of 'to be'. But, psycholinguists have suggested, the child always uses 'to be' in such sentences: it is just that it is sometimes deleted, transformationally, from the utterance.[1] Hence the child's speech is regular after all. But this sounds, to me, to be simply forcing a regularity upon the child's speech. At the very least, we should demand the evidence that could make us prefer to think that the child uses, but deletes, the verb instead of not using it at all.

Third, there is the danger that a regularity will be construed as a rule despite the fact that prior to the formulation of the rule there was no warrant for criticizing deviations from the regularity. Again, we would be inventing, not discovering, a rule. McNeill, for example, points out that children often omit the verb, though not the noun phrase, from the verb phrase containing them. For instance, the child who is supposedly expressing what we would express by 'Adam wants Mummy's pencil' will often say 'Adam Mummy's pencil' but not 'Adam wants'. McNeill interprets this as showing that

> the verb of the VP in this grammar is optional, while the noun of the VP is obligatory. Other children obey the same strange rule (1970 : p. 28).

But the notion of a rule is idle here. What is added to the information that children often leave out the verb by saying that they are following the rule VP → (V) NP (where the parentheses express the optionality of V)? Certainly it is not that we, or other children, criticize the leaving out of the noun phrase in a way that we do not criticize the leaving out of the verb. 'Optional' seems to mean no more than irregular, and 'obligatory' no more than regular.

To overlook these and other dangers is, as I have said, to invite an exaggerated picture of the extent to which language is rule-governed. But, having mentioned them, I don't want to deny there are any number of regularities which we can treat as rules, in that deviation from them results in ungrammaticality, meaninglessness, or whatever.

It is one thing to admit there are rules of language and quite another to admit that speakers follow these in their speech, even when their speech is grammatical and meaningful. Rule-following is not the same as rule-accordance. A child writing down the 2X multiplication table correctly is producing results that accord with axioms of set theory; but if he is following the method of simply looking over the shoulder of the boy at the next desk and copying, then he is not following these axioms. A writer who puts 's' at the end of regular nouns when pluralizing them is acting in accordance with the rule 'Place the 19th letter of the English alphabet at the end of regular nouns to pluralize them', but he is not guiding his behaviour by that rule, nor following it. Indeed, it is impossible for a person to follow all the rules with which his behaviour is accordant. For take some rule that enjoins doing X. It will always be possible to construct another rule which also enjoins doing X but which contains, as an instruction, that one should avoid the method prescribed by the first rule. If he then does X, he will be doing something that accords with both rules, in that doing X is what is enjoined by both, yet he cannot have followed both.

What is it, then, to follow rules, to be guided by them? It will be useful to take a paradigm of linguistic behaviour which would clearly count as rule-following and rule-guided behaviour. A foreigner, almost totally ignorant of English, arranges to write letters in that language to an English pen-friend. He arms himself with an English grammar and a dictionary, and each sentence he writes is painfully constructed after due reference to the rules found in the books. He performs what we might call 'consultative acts'. He consults the rule books, selects a rule, and arranges the next step in the letter according to that rule.

Of course it would be unreasonable, and quite out of keeping with ordinary usage, to restrict the term 'rule-following' to just the kind of behaviour exhibited in this paradigm. As our foreigner gets used to composing letters in English, he will no longer need to look up the rules each time he writes another word or phrase down. He will remember them and consult them 'in his head'. Sooner or later it will become automatic for him to write one thing down rather than another, so that he no longer has to consult the rules even 'in his head'. But although he will no longer need to perform consultative acts generally, he is able to, and should the need arise, when he is unsure how to progress with some sentence, this is what he will do. Certainly we would want to say that his later behaviour is rule-following, for not only is he able to perform consultative acts but it is his past record of performing them that has put him in the position of writing letters without having to perform them.

I shall say that a person is rule-following $_1$ or rule-guided$_1$ if he behaves like our foreigner behaved, either in the original paradigm or later on, when he could still perform consultative acts though the need to do so has, in general, disappeared. For the moment I attach no particular significance to the numerical subscript. I leave it open whether rule-following$_1$ is the only kind of rule-following, or whether it is rule-following in a quite distinct sense from other kinds, if any.

It is clear that many philosophers, and all the linguists with whom we are concerned, take rule-following$_1$ to be included in a far wider range of rule-following behaviour. For native speakers obviously do not follow$_1$ the phrase structure rules and transformation rules of generative grammar. They are not even able, generally, to formulate these rules, let alone consult them and adjust their linguistic behaviour by explicit reference to them. Linguists may be able to formulate them, but they would rarely if ever consult them when producing sentences in everyday conversation. So, if rule-following$_1$ were the only form of rule-following, then speakers do not follow, and are not guided by, the rules of generative grammar. Thus a basic ingredient of KLT would be false.

What could it be, then, to follow rules without following$_1$ them? Slobin presents us with a fairly typical answer when he writes:

> We can be fairly sure that a child has some rule system if his production is regular, if he extends these regularities to new instances, and if he can detect deviations from regularity in his own speech and the speech of others. This is generally what psycholinguists mean when they speak of the child's learning or forming, or possession of linguistic rules . . . Explicit statement of rules is irrelevant to our concerns here and is an entirely different sort of ability (pp. 54-5).

Somewhat more formally, the claim runs that a person is following a rule R if

i   his behaviour regularly conforms to R
ii   his regular, R-conforming behaviour, is extended in new cases, and
iii   he criticizes deviations from R.

Clause (ii) is required to distinguish the rule-follower's behaviour from the regular behaviour of someone who is imitating or conforming out of luck. Clause (iii) is taken as crucial. Max Black, for example, grounds his claim that speakers follow 'implicit rules' on their 'readiness to correct themselves and others' (p. 136). And another writer remarks:

> There is this characteristic difference between our reactions to rule-governed regularities and our reactions to variations from regularities which are not rule-governed; we correct the former though not the latter (Snyder : p. 19).

Let us say that a person who behaves in the ways specified by clauses (i) to (iii) exhibits rule-following behaviour (RFB). And let us say that a person who exhibits RFB but is not following$_1$ rules is rule-following$_2$ or rule-guided$_2$. Proponents of KLT will then hold that speakers follow$_2$ the rules of a generative grammar, even though they don't follow$_1$ them.

For they regularly conform to them, even on occasions of 'novel' utterances; and they do criticize deviations from them as being ungrammatical, meaningless, garbled, and so on. Of course, they do not criticize deviations *for* transgressing this or that rule, for that would imply they could formulate the rules, in which case they would be rule-following$_1$. But this, as Slobin insists, is irrelevant to their counting as rule-followers.

Typically, those who regard rule-following$_2$ as a genuine species of rule-following will elaborate their position by defending it against various objections. Faced by the objection that rule-followers$_2$ do not formulate the rules in question, the tactic will be to produce examples where, despite the absence of explicit formulation, we should *surely* want to speak of rule-following. Black, for instance, imagines a tribe who do often follow explicitly formulated rules, and who in addition display all the signs of following a rule that we would formulate as 'Nobody shall touch the sacred fence'. But the tribesmen do not formulate this rule, since 'the whole affair is regarded as too holy for discussion' (p. 129). Black concludes that, despite this, we should surely want to describe them as following the rule in question. Faced by the objection that rule-following$_2$ is *merely* regular behaviour, and not genuinely rule-guided, the manoeuvre will be, first, to stress clause (iii), and second, to insist that there are regularities and regularities — both *mere* ones and others. It will be argued, for instance, that speaking in regular ways is not the only regularity we find in language. In addition, speakers regularly expect their brethren to speak in certain ways, and they regularly prefer them to speak in certain ways. Further, they expect their brethren to expect them to speak in certain ways, and expect their brethren to expect that they expect their brethren to speak in certain ways, and so on. And behaviour shot through with these multiple and mutual expectations and preferences is just what we count as conventional behaviour.[2] And conventional behaviour, where there are rules to be followed, is rule-following behaviour. So, in a sense, there are only regularities; but not all of them are mere ones, if that implies they are not also rules.

Well, I am reasonably happy to go along with all of this,[3] and to grant that rule-followers$_2$ are genuine rule-followers. It would not be mere stipulation to treat them as such. However, matters are by no means settled in favour of KLT. For the question remains wide open as to whether the sense or way in which rule-followers$_2$ follow rules is one which can support any of the claims made, or inferences drawn, by proponents of that thesis. Here are three typical claims made about rule-followers$_2$ by that thesis:

1   They 'hypothesize' the rules which they follow, and 'test' them against linguistic data.
2   They follow the rules 'unconsciously', 'tacitly', and 'implicitly'.
3   Their following the rules explains their linguistic behaviour, partially at least.

(The behaviour mentioned in (3) is what we called RFG — regularities in speech, criticism of deviations from these regularities, and so on). The question is, could any of these claims about rule-followers$_2$ make sense? If not, the cause of KLT has not been advanced, since it is admitted that speakers do not follow$_1$ the rules of generative grammar.

We will approach this question by looking at the relation between rule-following$_1$ and rule-following$_2$. It is, I think, generally conceded that the propriety of describing rule-following$_2$ as genuine rule-following derives from its relation with rule-following$_1$ which, after all, provides us with our paradigm. Waismann writes in connection with persons spoken of as following rules they are unable to formulate:

> Only where there is sufficient similarity to actions that proceed according to explicitly stated rules is this manner of speaking appropriate (p. 135).

Rule-following$_2$, we might say, is rule-following in virtue of its analogy with rule-following$_1$. Consequently the argument for treating rule-following$_2$ as genuine rule-following is an argument from analogy.

Arguments from analogy, however, can be of (at least) two very different types. First, there is what might be called 'argument from analogical *inference*'. This is exemplified by the old argument from design. Since complicated bits of machinery have human makers, it is reasonable to infer that things which are like complicated bits of machinery, flowers for example, have a human-like maker, God. Or, to take another exemplification: since I behave in certain ways when I feel pain, it is reasonable to infer that creatures which behave like me also feel something like I do. Applied to what concerns us, the argument would run: since persons (i.e. rule-followers$_1$) who consult rules and adjust their speech by reference to these behave in certain ways (i.e. they exhibit RFB), then it is reasonable to infer that other persons who behave in these ways are doing something closely analogous to consulting rules and adjusting their speech by reference to them. These 'other persons' are rule-followers$_2$, and what makes them rule-followers is that it is reasonable to infer they do something, in addition to exhibiting RFB, which is very like what rule-followers$_i$ do. Of course, they do not do *just* the same as rule-followers$_1$, since they cannot formulate their rules. But this lack of explicit awareness is the sole difference between them and rule-followers$_1$.

Second, there is what has been called 'argument from analogical *extension*'. This is exemplified by various arguments in Geach's *Mental Acts* and, perhaps, of Wittgenstein. Since animals behave in ways which bear some resemblance to the ways we behave when we make judgments, it is reasonable, or at least intelligible, to extend the description 'making judgments' to animals. It is the behaviour alone, not any inference from this to the occurrence of animal mental acts corresponding to human ones, that warrants the extension of the description. Again, a person who skips is behaving, in some ways, similarly to a footballer, and this similarity makes it reasonable or intelligible to describe him as playing a game. It is just this similarity in behaviour or setting which warrants the extension, not any inference from this to the skipper's doing something else which is the same as a footballer. Applied to rule-following, the argument would be: in several respects (i.e. RFB) the behaviour of rule-followers$_1$ is matched by other persons. Hence it is reasonable or intelligible to extend the description 'following rules' to these others, the rule-followers$_2$. That this is so is not due to any further similarity between rule-followers$_1$ and rule-followers$_2$ which could be inferred from RFB.

I think it is clear that proponents of KLT are using the first kind of argument, the one from analogical inference. For they judge speakers who exhibit RFB to be following rules on the ground that it is reasonable to infer from this behaviour that they are doing something analogous to what rule-followers$_1$ are doing. It is only if they are arguing in this way that I can make sense of the frequent claims to the effect that RFB provides *evidence* or *clues* for rule-following. Slobin, for example, prefaces the passage quoted on p. 44 by saying that the behaviour described in it is 'evidence for rules' and the following of rules by children. And McNeill regards the regularities in the child's 'telegraphic' or 'pivot-open' speech as 'evidence' for his organizing utterances 'according to definite principles' (1970 : p. 19). If rule-followers$_2$ were following rules simply by virtue of their exhibiting RFB, this talk of evidence would be out of place. As Waismann, echoing Wittgenstein, stresses, there is all the difference between treating such behaviour as symptomatic of rule-following and treating it as the criterion for a certain kind of rule-following. To argue by analogical inference is to treat RFB as symptomatic; to argue by analogical extension is to treat it as criterial.

If RFB is evidence for rule-following, we can ask just what it is evidence for. Presumably it is evidence for the fact that rule-followers$_2$ do something, in addition to exhibiting such behaviour, analogous to that of rule-followers$_1$. And when we turn to descriptions of rule-following$_2$ in KLT, it becomes clear that its proponents have just this in mind. Chomsky, for example, refers to the 'mental representations and interpretative operations' which speakers engage in when speaking in accordance with a 'sequence of rules' — though they are not such as one could 'hope to determine . . . by introspection' (1970 : p. 438). So just as rule-followers$_1$ represent rules to themselves, by looking them up in a book or just reminding themselves of them, and just as they 'operate' by consulting these rules, so rule-followers$_2$ do likewise — with the difference that they are not aware of what they are doing or of the rules involved. And Katz accounts for sentence-production in terms of 'processes going on inside the speaker's head', such as running through 'the sentence production procedure to obtain an abstract syntactic structure, (1967 : pp. 80-1). This sounds like a description of what our original foreigner might be doing when composing his letters in English. And, indeed, the only way Katz's speaker differs is that the processes going on in his head are not 'open to . . . (his) conscious awareness'. Katz in fact emphasizes that his model of sentence-production is 'phrased as if the processes described were conscious' (p. 81).

Put simply — or oversimply — speakers follow$_2$ rules, according to KLT, because the behaviour they exhibit is evidence for their engaging in the sort of mental processes and acts which rule-followers$_1$ do or can engage in — consulting a set of rules, selecting one, adjusting steps by reference to it, and so on. The only difference between rule-followers$_2$ and rule-followers$_1$ is that the former are not aware of what it is they are doing. We might dub this the 'process/act' view of rule-following$_2$. And we can contrast this with what we might call the 'behavioural' view, arrived at by an argument from analogical extension. On this latter view, speculation as to the mental processes and acts rule-followers$_2$ might be engaged in has no relevance for treating them as genuine rule-followers. Reference to such processes and acts plays no part in explaining or justifying the description of them as rule-followers. They follow rules simply by virtue of exhibiting RFB.

It is important to see that proponents of KLT not only do, but must, take the 'process/act' view of rule-following$_2$. For it is only then that claims like (1) to (3) (see p. 46) can make sense, or the appropriate sense. It was claimed first, remember, that rule-followers$_2$, at least in their early days, hypothesize as to the nature of the rules of grammar, and test their hypotheses against the data encountered in their linguistic environment. Now this could indeed be the sort of thing our rule-following$_1$ letter writer was doing. He guesses at a rule, constructs a sentence in accordance with it, and tests his guess by the response of his English pen-friend. But if rule-followers$_2$ are simply those who exhibit RFB, then such operations of hypothesizing and testing are no part of their following rules. Second, rule-followers$_2$ were said to be following the rules of grammar 'unconsciously' or 'tacitly'. Now if rule-following$_2$ were simply exhibiting RFB, it is not clear what this could mean. I suppose we might imagine a man who spoke in regular ways and who criticized deviations from his normal regularities, but who was generally unaware of doing any of this. So perhaps someone who talks in his sleep, and in self-correcting ways at that, would be unconsciously exhibiting RFB, and thus unconsciously following$_2$ rules. But it is plain that this is not what is intended by 'unconscious rule-following' by KLT. For one thing, very few if any persons unconsciously follow rules in the sense just described, whereas all speakers most of the time are supposed to be unconsciously following rules according to KLT. (See note 2 to chapter 2). For that claim to make sense, or at any rate be true, one has to suppose that rule-followers$_2$ are doing something, other than exhibiting RFB, which is very like what rule-followers$_1$ do — representing rules to themselves, selecting them, judging their applicability in some instance, etc. — only without any awareness of these processes and acts.

Finally, the fact that speakers follow rules was meant to explain (partly) their linguistic behaviour, especially that behaviour we have called RFB. It is supposed to be because they are following the rule for passivization, say, that they correct ill-formed passive sentences. But if rule-following$_2$ were simply exhibiting RFB, it could not be used to explain RFB — not in the intended sense, at least. Perhaps there is a sense of 'explain' in which rule-following$_2$ would explain RFB even when identified with RFB. Tautologies can explain, I suppose, in the sense of characterizing behaviour in appropriate ways. (See chapter 7). But, for KLT, the claim that following rules explains RFB is not intended as a tautology or conceptual truth. The explanation in question is meant to be of some causal variety. According to Katz, the view that speakers follow the rules of a generative grammar is part of a

theory that . . . explains the facts of linguistic communication by showing them to be behavioural consequences of
the operation of a mechanism with just the structure that
the formulated theory attributes to it (1967 : p. 76).

For the proponent of KLT, then, the claim that people who
exhibit RFB are following rules is an empirical one, and to be
contrasted with such views as that the behaviour is 'imitative',
'conditioned', 'merely' dispositional, chance, and so on. Once
more, the claim only makes sense if rule-following$_2$ is thought
to involve mental processes and acts analogous to those
involved in rule-following$_1$. For it is indeed true that the
consultative acts of our foreigner do, as a matter of empirical
fact, explain his subsequent letter writing in some causal
manner.

So, proponents of KLT not only do, but must, take a certain view about rule-following$_2$ — the 'process/act' view based
on an argument from analogical inference.

So far I have simply stated, without assessment, the two
kinds of analogical argument and the two resulting concep-
tions of what is involved in rule-following$_2$. In the remainder
of this chapter I want to go some of the way towards rejection of the 'process/act' view and the argument on which it
rests. Not all of the way, since residual questions — about
unconscious knowledge, for example, or the explanation of
'creativity' — are deferred. Since, as we have seen, KLT
incorporates the 'process/act' view, we shall though be going
some of the way towards rejection of that thesis.

Much of the case against the 'process/act' view is made
once it is realized that there is an alternative way of conceiving
of rule-following$_2$. If the 'process/act' view were the only
respectable one, then all proponents of KLT would need do is
force the admission that speakers follow rules. And that is
something, it seems, which has to be admitted. We seem thrust
towards KLT. But the thrust is blocked once it is seen that
we can admit speakers to be rule-followers without accepting
the implications drawn by proponents of KLT. And this is
possible if speakers are, by analogical extension, regarded as
rule-followers simply by virtue of exhibiting RFB. The onus

will now have shifted. At first, seemingly, it was we opponents of KLT who were being forced into the unfortunate position of having to deny that any but rule-followers$_1$ are genuinely following rules. Now the onus is upon proponents of KLT to show why rule-followers$_2$ must be following rules in the 'process/act' sense rather than by just exhibiting RFB. The onus is theirs for, surely, we opponents are on the right side of Occam's razor here. That explanation of why rule-followers$_2$ are genuine rule-followers is to be preferred which, if sufficient, is minimally contentious. And it is more contentious to claim that rule-followers$_2$ do something analogous to rule-followers$_1$, in addition to exhibiting RFB, than to claim simply that they exhibit RFB. But the latter claim is, seemingly, all that is required to justify treating speakers as genuinely following rules. To recall an earlier analogy: if we can make our talk of animals making judgments intelligible without supposing that they perform the mental acts you and I perform when we assert things, then we should not suppose this. For one thing, unwelcome questions like 'What is the animal analogue to the words humans employ when asserting things?' are bypassed. I take it that some of Wittgenstein's case against 'privacy' consists in showing how we can explain what we want to explain, or make sense of the ways in which we talk, without appealing to it. The same case — and more — operates against the ‹conception of rule-following to which KLT is committed.

Turning to actual objections to the 'process/act' view, one which is bound to arise is as follows: How and in what sense can the processes or acts engaged in or performed by rule-followers$_2$ be *like* those involved in rule-following$_1$? What is it to do something like looking up a rule on p. 25 of a grammar book, checking to see that one's proposed sentence does not violate it, or proceeding at each step in accordance with its explicit instructions? Well, I suppose rifling one's memory for rules one has learned, and proceeding according to one that comes to mind, would be relevantly similar. And so, I suppose, would consulting a more knowledgeable friend and acting on his instructions. But any such procedures are ones of which the agents are straightforwardly conscious. They could tell you what they are doing — and if they could not, why suppose they are doing it? Perhaps we can even lend sense to doing this sort of thing unconsciously. Our foreigner, with his letter preying on his mind as he goes to bed, might get up in his sleep and, zombie-like, flick through the pages of his grammar book. But this case would not remotely approximate to those that proponents of KLT must have in mind. For them, our rule-consulting acts go on when we are wide awake, and when we are (in general) able to answer questions about the things we have been doing. Yet we have no grammar book at hand, no friends to consult, and no awareness of being engaged in any such consultative acts. I do not want to press this line of argument too hard for the present. For I am aware of possible counters — such as that the processes going on 'in the heads' of rule-followers$_2$ are like the ones engaged in by rule-followers$_1$ by virtue of their 'functional equivalence'. More about this, and about the problems of unconsciousness, in the following chapter. But, *prima facie,* the 'process/act' view faces a huge difficulty in illuminating the nature of the mental activity which rule-followers$_2$ are allegedly engaged in.

The most telling objection to comparing rule-following$_2$ with rule-following$_1$, beyond the admitted similarity in RFB, is of a quite different sort. If a person's behaviour accords with a rule then it also accords with any other rule which is, as we might put it, 'extensionally equivalent' to the first. In calling two rules extensionally equivalent I mean, first, that they (or rather their descriptions) are not synonymous, and second, that whatever behaviour deviates from what is enjoined by the one rule also deviates from what is enjoined by the second. So, for example, the rules 'Write down 's' whenever. . . . ' and 'Write down the 19th letter of the English alphabet whenever. . . . ' are extensionally equivalent. More interestingly, if a grammar is thought of as comprising a set of axioms, then there must be any number of extensionally equivalent grammars; for it is truistic that whatever can be axiomatized at all can be axiomatized in any number of different ways. Not only could there be competing transformational grammars having, as output, the same class of well-formed sentences, but it is possible to devise grammars of a quite different kind (perhaps a phrase structure kind) which also have that output.[4]

If a person is following₁ a rule, however, it certainly cannot be inferred that he is following₁ another rule extensionally equivalent to it. Our foreigner who is following₁ the rules of one grammar book is not following₁ the rules of a rival one. Indeed, it can make no sense to suppose that rule-followers₁ are following₁ the rules of two different, but extensionally equivalent, sets. For we identified our foreigner as as a rule-follower₁ precisely because he was consulting certain rules in a certain book and not others, or being given certain rules by his friend and not others. It is necessarily the case with rule-followers₁ that we can, in principle, identify *which* rules they are following, or that the question 'Which of the extensionally equivalent rules are they now following, and which not?' is sensible.

Now if rule-following₂ is simply exhibiting RFB we could not identify which of some extensionally equivalent rules the speakers are following. And this will be not because we lack information, but because there is no sense to be lent to the supposition that some rather than other rules are being followed. For if following a rule R is simply to be acting regularly under some description 'R', then it is equally to be acting regularly under the descriptions 'R1', 'R2' . . . 'Rn', where 'R' . . . 'Rn' are extensionally equivalent descriptions. Hence following R would, *ipso facto,* be to follow R1 . . . Rn as well. The point is that RFB alone can never determine which of the extensionally equivalent rules a speaker is following. Rating sentences for grammaticality or well-formedness, which is included in RFB, will not, for example, suffice. As Quine remarks, 'extensionally equivalent rules are indistinguishable on that score' (1970 : p. 388). For whatever is ill-formed through violation of some rule R will also be ill-formed through violations of the extensionally equivalent rules R1 . . . Rn.

The problem for KLT, or for the 'process/act' view, should now be emerging. It is admitted by those who hold that thesis or view that the only evidence for supposing that speakers follow rules is that provided by RFB. Yet, we see, RFB alone can never determine which rules are being followed, or even provide the grounds for sensibly supposing that some rather than others are being followed. It is no use saying that the rules being followed are the 'right' ones or the 'descriptively adequate' ones[5]. In one sense, a rule is the 'right' one or 'descriptively adequate' if it captures a regularity in RFB (or in some 'idealized' segment of RFB). But, in this sense, all extensionally equivalent rules are as 'right' or 'descriptively adequate' as one another. For, to repeat, whatever behaviour conforms with a rule R also conforms with R1 . . . Rn where these are all extensionally equivalent. If, on the other hand, the 'right' and 'descriptively adequate' rules are understood as those which the speaker has actually 'internalized', or 'tacitly' knows, or in fact employs in his 'sentence production procedure', then the question is begged. Whether there are such rules, and whether it even makes sense to suppose there are, is precisely what is being challenged.

Nor will there be any use in pointing out that it is *sometimes* sensible and justifiable to infer from RFB as to which out of some extensionally equivalent rules a speaker is following. Certainly it sometimes is. Suppose we have observed all the boys in a language class, except for one who is away sick, producing foreign sentences by consulting a grammar book prescribed by their teacher. We then notice that the missing boy's work-book contains sentences and jottings very like those we have observed the other boys putting down. It will then be perfectly reasonable to infer that he, like they, has been following the same rules in the same grammar book. But this inference depends upon our having encountered cases where we know, directly, that RFB results from consulting and following certain rules rather than others. If we had not observed what the rest of the boys were doing, we should have had no right for inferring what the missing boy has been doing. This situation does not obtain when we turn to fluent, native speakers following the rules of a generative grammar. For, of course, we do not find native speakers consulting the rules of, say, Chomsky's *Aspects of the Theory of Syntax* when uttering their everyday sentences. We might, I suppose, catch occasional eccentric linguists explicitly consulting rules when speaking. But there is no reason to think they would be consulting the same ones, and even if they did, they need not.

Either way there would be no warrant for inferring what the rest of the population might be doing.

Nor, finally, is it any good replying along these lines:

> Look, all you have shown is that *we* can not tell which rule a speaker is following out of some extensionally equivalent ones. This does not mean that he is not following one rather than the others.

This reply suggests that our problem is like the one we might face in the following situation: a drowned foreigner is washed up on a beach, and in his pockets are note-books full of painfully constructed English sentences. We wonder which system of English teaching for foreigners he has been through, which rules from which books he has been consulting. Certainly it is reasonable to think he has been through some such system, only we cannot find out which, for we have no way of identifying the body or the school from which he comes. We are forever ignorant of which rules he has been following, though we can be sure he has been following some, not others. But this situation, of course, is totally different from the situation vis-á-vis fluent, native speakers. In the case of the drowned man we are prevented by various contingent circumstances from getting the answer we want. But with fluent, native speakers we have no idea what it is we are looking for. It is not that we are prevented, through contingent limitations, from discovering *further* evidence — analogous to finding out the school our drowned man attended in his own country. There is no evidence, beyond RFB, to look for. And RFB, as we have seen, can determine nothing. Or, we might put things like this: we identified our original foreigner as a rule-follower$_1$ through observing that he performed certain consultative acts when composing his letters. And we could observe that only through identifying the rules — in his grammar book, or as recited by him from memory — which he was consulting. Now we might, if he had been very secretive, have been unable to do this. Still, since *he* would have been aware of what he was doing, we could nevertheless count him as a rule-follower$_1$. But once we admit that there is no way of telling — either for us or for the speaker — which rules are being followed, what sense is left in the reference to consultative acts; acts which are identifiable only on the basis of identification of the rules being consulted? None. So the claim that the speaker is following certain rules, or performing certain consultative acts, despite the fact that no one, including him, can tell which, is an idle one. The conditions in terms of which it makes sense to speak of such rule-following and acts have been removed. Hence the claim that rule-followers$_2$ are doing something analogous to rule-followers$_1$, in addition to exhibiting RFB, is also idle. The very condition that makes rule-following$_1$, what it is — the identifiability of which out of some extensionally equivalent rules is being followed — is missing in the case of rule-following$_2$. Apart from RFB, rule-following$_2$ is irretrievably disanalogous to rule-following$_1$.

The topic of this chapter, as I said, is by no means finished with. But for the moment it is safe to say we have found no strong reason for, and several strong reasons against, accepting that model of rule-following which alone can support the conclusions of KLT.

Notes to chapter 3

1   See McNeill (1970 : circa p. 33).

2   See Lewis for an excellent discussion of conventions and rules along these lines.

3   I go along with it despite the shakiness of some of the supporting considerations. For instance, Black's example of the tribesmen who do not explicitly formulate their rule about not touching the sacred fence, seems to me to be an example of rule-following$_1$, not of some different kind of 'implicit' rule-following. True, the tribesmen do not actually mention the rule, but this is not because they are unable to, but because it is 'too holy' to mention publicly.

4   For more on extensionally equivalent axiomatic systems, including grammars, see Stich (1972) and Harman (1968-9a).

5   For the notion of 'descriptive adequacy', see Chomsky (1965 : chapter 1). See also chapter 5 below.

Chapter 4

Knowledge of Grammar

To say that a person knows the rules he is following is to say more than that he is simply following them. He may only be following₂ them. A foreigner may come to know what the rules of our road are long after he began to follow₂ them in his rented car from the airport. So, to show that speakers have knowledge of rules requires more than the demonstration that they follow them. This is one reason for treating knowledge in a separate chapter.

In the last chapter we rejected the objectionable 'process/act' view of rule-following₂ which KLT presupposes, but we did leave open the bare possibility that this view might be re-scaffolded in the light of an acceptable and intelligible account of unconscious knowledge. So let us see if anything can be made of that bare possibility. A final reason for treating of knowledge in a separate chapter from rules is that, for KLT, speakers' knowledge is by no means confined to rules, so that it is not obvious if our criticisms of the objectionable view of rule-following would damage other elements in KLT.

In addition to the rules of a generative grammar, fluent speakers are said to have knowledge of the categories, structures, relations, and definitions of such a grammar. When, for example, a speaker understands the sentence 'Flying planes can be dangerous' to be ambiguous, at least the following knowledge is ascribed to him: knowledge of (a) the two deep structures underlying the sentence, (b) the transformation rules relating these structures to the sentence, (c) the phrase structure rules employed in the derivation of the underlying strings, (d) the grammatical categories of NP and VP, (e) the grammatical relations Subject, Predicate, and Object, and (f) the definitions of these relations in terms of categories (e.g. Subject = df. Leftmost NP in the deep structure).

The logical form(s) of expressions like 'knowledge of rules' or 'knowledge of grammatical categories' is not entirely obvious. But I take it they are equivalent to certain expressions containing 'knowledge that'. To say, for example, that a person knows the rule for passivization is to say he knows that the rule is. . . . To say he knows the categories of grammar is to say he knows that the categories are. . . . Casting expressions like 'knowledge of rules' in this way suggests, no doubt, a certain view of what the knowledge is like — but it is a view, I think, that proponents of KLT must be taking. For, as we saw in chapter 1, the knowledge in question cannot be mere know *how*; it must be of a type which can sensibly be described as 'unconscious' or 'tacit', which can serve to explain linguistic behaviour in an empirical manner, and which is 'psychologically real' or 'mentally represented'.

Unfortunately, and confusingly, Chomsky has denied that the knowledge of rules, structures, etc. that he postulates takes the form of knowledge *that* the rules or structures are. . . . He takes Harman, for example, to task for attributing such a view to him. However, what Chomsky is really denying here is that the knowledge in question is of a type that speakers can state and formulate.

> Obviously, it is absurd to suppose that the speaker of the language knows the rules in the sense of being able to state them (1969 : p. 86).

But it would be disingenuous for him to deny that the knowledge is describable as knowledge *that,* once the objectionable implication of explicit formulatability is removed, since in any number of places this is just how he does describe it. Harman, assiduously, has counted no less than fifteen places in *Aspects of the Theory of Syntax* where Chomsky does this (1967). And we have already encountered this mode of speaking on several occasions (for example, in his explanation of the speaker's recognition that a question is ill-formed because he knows that a certain structure-dependent rule has not been utilized. (see p. 24)). At any rate when *I* say that the knowledge postulated by KLT is knowledge *that*, I am not making the 'absurd suggestion' that it is knowledge which the speaker is able to state or formulate. I insist on treating the postulated knowledge in this way partly because this is how Chomsky and others generally describe it, and partly in order to contrast it with knowledge of the know *how* variety which cannot be intended by them. To take, by way of illustration, just one passage which would be difficult to interpret unless the postulated knowledge is treated in the above way:

> . . . speaking a language requires information about the structural relations within and among the sentences of that language . . . the speaker's ability to produce coherent utterances depends upon his exploitation of knowledge about transition probabilities between elements of his language (Fodor 1966 : p. 105).

The first, and main, task in this chapter will be to assess the claim that there is grammatical knowledge of the above kind. But there is a second, and by no means unimportant, issue taken up towards the end. Until then we shall have been talking about knowledge but not knowledge in contrast to belief, assumption, thinking, and other epistemic notions. Most of the problems in deciding if there could be grammatical knowledge of the proposed type would also be problems in deciding if speakers could have beliefs about, or make assumptions about, or possess information about their grammars. There are, though, special problems with the claim that it is knowledge not mere belief etc. that speakers have vis-á-vis their grammars. And the interest of these problems extends well beyond their connection with KLT.

What could justify postulating grammatical knowledge of the type sketched? Granted that it is not of the paradigmatic kind that persons do or can avow, then as Stich asks 'are there any extenuating circumstances, any facts which justify the attribution of knowledge in spite of the evident dissimilarities to more standard cases of knowledge?' (1971 : p. 488).

Remarkably little has been said by psycholinguists and

philosophers in support of their postulate. Fodor, for instance, prefaces the passage recently quoted by saying it expresses something which is 'beyond dispute'. And, generally, it seems to be taken either as self-evident, or a matter of more-or-less arbitrary decision, that there is knowledge of the type proposed by KLT. But to take the first view is to ignore the obvious dissimilarities there are between uncontroversial cases of knowledge and the cases being proposed. It will not do to say 'that the argument that we should extend the explanation (i.e. explanation in terms of people's knowledge) is simply that by doing so we explain' linguistic intuitions and behaviour (Graves, Katz et. al. : p. 325). For the challenge which has been laid down is to make sense of this extended, controversial talk of grammatical knowledge. Until that is done, no question can arise as to the explanatory value, or lack of it, of the postulated knowledge. To take the second view — that it is a matter of arbitrary decision whether we extend our talk of knowledge in the proposed manner — is, as remarked on p. 4 in connection with innate knowledge, to eschew interest in most of the philosophical questions involved. Perhaps psycholinguists are not hindered in their empirical work by a decision to speak in these new ways, but as philosophers we can question that decision.

Although little has been said by way of support, it is possible to guess what the justification for postulating grammatical knowledge of the relevant type might be. And sometimes, if rarely, the justification is explicitly attempted. It runs something like this:

A person's knowledge (belief, assumption, etc.) that P is a state which brings about certain behaviour in that person. Indeed, the item of knowledge is typically identified on the basis of the behaviour it brings about. Now states which bring about equivalent sorts of behaviour are the same states, in some relevant sense of 'same'. So, if a person who knows that P behaves, as a result, in manner B, then other persons who behave in manner B must, other explanations failing, be in the same state as him, and hence know that P. This is so even if they are not aware that P and would not avow that they know P. A state, to be one describable as 'knowing that P', does not have to be one the person is conscious of being in. All that is required is that it be 'functionally equivalent', equivalent in the role played in bringing about behaviour, to a state of which a person is or might be conscious of being in.

Let us call this the 'functional' doctrine.

Fodor is taking this line when he writes:

> . . . the criteria employed for individuating (psychological) constructs are based primarily upon hypotheses about the role they play in the aetiology of behaviour (1968b : pp. 107-8).

He goes on to imply that awareness and avowability are inessential for a person to be described as knowing, believing, etc. that P, since he says it would be 'an irrational policy' to deny that machines which simulate human behaviour think. They are in states functionally equivalent to those of human beings, and that is the relevant thing. A 'functional' doctrine can also be found in Armstrong's *A Materialist Theory of Mind.* Beliefs, or 'logically fundamental' ones at any rate, are 'mental states apt for selective behaviour towards the environment' (p. 339). Knowledge is then defined in terms of beliefs. It follows, says Armstrong, that knowledge need not be conscious; one may not know that one knows. For it is quite possible that a person should be in a state apt for producing certain behaviour without realizing he is. Armstrong, in the spirit of his book's title, goes on to identify the difference between conscious and non-conscious knowledge with a brain's scanning and not scanning its own states — but this claim is not essential to the doctrine as it will concern us.

So the answer to our question 'What justifies postulating ordinary speakers' non-trivial knowledge of a grammar?' is supposed to be: they behave in those ways — including producing and understanding new sentences, or making judgments about them — that persons who were explicitly aware of, and ready to avow, information about the nature of a grammar would behave. More briefly, ordinary speakers must be in states which are functionally equivalent to those that persons who uncontroversially have the knowledge in question would be in (if there were any). Since it is function, effect upon behaviour, which identifies states as ones of knowledge or belief, there can be no good reason to deny that ordinary speakers possess the relevant knowledge or beliefs. Since, for example, fluent speakers often produce and understand and judge as well-formed strings like 'the fat boy' or 'the old man', then they are behaving in the way that a person who knew, in some quite uncontroversial sense, that NP → Det. + Adj. + N is a rule of English would behave. Hence they too know this is a rule of English.

No doubt, this 'functional' doctrine would have to be tightened in a number of ways if some obvious queries and objections are to be avoided. For instance, we should certainly want to be told *how* similar the behaviour of two people has to be before they can be said to be in functionally equivalent states. For, clearly, there is some behaviour which only the person who uncontroversially knows that P will exhibit — avowing this knowledge, for instance, or objecting to someone he hears denying 'P'. So, functionally equivalent states cannot be intended as ones which result in exactly the same behaviour. I shall assume that problems like this can be overcome, that the notion of 'functionally equivalent states' can be intelligibly presented. Nor shall I be concerned to question the challengeable assumption that knowledge and belief *cause* the behaviour which serves to identify them as the states they are. For I want to face directly and squarely the question of whether we have been given a genuine justification for extending our talk of knowledge and belief in the required way. Granted that a fluent speaker is in a state functionally equivalent to that of a person who might, in some uncontroversial sense, know the rules, structures, categories, etc. of a grammar, but is this sufficient to establish that the fluent speaker likewise knows a grammar?

I shall answer these questions negatively. My objections to the alleged justification appear in order of increasing importance.

1. It is crucial to the 'functional' doctrine that it permits and specifies a clear distinction between 'conscious' ('expli-

cit', etc.) knowledge and belief, and 'unconscious' ('implicit', 'tacit', etc.) knowledge and belief. Indeed, its strength was supposed to reside precisely in doing these things. Now one presumes that the above distinction is meant to be equivalent to the distinction between awareness of, and lack of awareness of, being in a state apt to produce certain behaviour. For the natural way to read 'He is aware that he knows that P', by the 'functional' view, would be 'He is aware that he is in a state apt. . . .etc. . . ' . For this reading results when we replace 'knows' in the first sentence by its alleged definiens (see Armstrong's definition of 'belief' on p. 62). Likewise, a person who is not aware that he knows that P is someone who is not aware that he is in a state apt. . . .etc. . . . But, while this distinction between being and not being aware of states apt for producing behaviour may be a genuine enough one, I cannot see that it is faintly equivalent to any that could be drawn between 'conscious' and unconscious' knowledge or belief, in any normal sense of these terms.

First, 'He is aware that he knows that P' could not normally be taken to mean that he is aware of being in a state apt. . . .etc. . . . If this were normally meant then, I am afraid, we are usually mistaken in supposing that men are aware of what they know. A man, let us suppose, knows that his wife ruined his career, and from the conviction with which he affirms this we can tell he is well aware of the fact. But need he be aware which of his behaviour this knowledge has resulted in and been responsible for? And need he be aware what sort of behaviour such knowledge is typically apt for producing? Let us take the second question. No doubt he will be aware that certain behaviour would typically be explained by such knowledge — such verbal behaviour, for example, as saying 'My wife ruined my career'. But behaviour of this sort, avowal behaviour, cannot of course be included within the 'functional' doctrine. The only type that can be included is behaviour which can be shared by those who do and those who do not avow their knowledge and beliefs. But, then, I see no reason to think our unfortunate husband should have to be aware of the behaviour, other than avowal behaviour, that knowing one's wife ruined one's career typically results in.

This would imply a certain amount of worldly and sociological knowledge on his part that could not be inferred from the bare claim that he knows *his* wife ruined *his* career. Nor, as far as I can see, need he be aware which of his hostile behaviour towards his wife has resulted from knowing she ruined his career, as distinct from his knowing she has been unfaithful to him, or from his general mysogeny. People, as we know, are often unaware of what motivates or causes their behaviour; and this includes being unaware of what roles various of their beliefs might have played. Being aware that one is in a state apt for producing certain behaviour cannot, then, be necessary for knowing, with full awareness, that P.

Nor, is it sufficient. Suppose a man is consistently able to discriminate between red and yellow objects. He is in a state, then, which produces certain discriminatory behaviour. So let us grant, for the sake of argument at least, that he knows the difference between red and yellow, or that red and yellow are different colours. Further, he is well aware of being in a state apt for producing such behaviour; he is well aware, that is, of his ability to sort out objects of the two different colours. Does it follow that he is aware of knowing the difference between yellow and red? In the only sense I can imagine these words could tolerably bear, the answer is 'No'. Imagine he had been trained to call by the name 'yellow' what is in fact a particular shade of red, and to call what are in fact yellow things 'blue', and what are in fact red (in general) 'green'. In that case, he would, presumably, deny that he is discriminating between yellow and red, since according to him these are not different colours at all; rather, one is a shade of the other. He would insist instead that he is discriminating between blue and green. Under these circumstances, it could well be strange to describe him as being aware of knowing the difference between yellow and red, despite the fact that he is aware of being in a state apt to produce the same behaviour as that of a man who is aware of knowing the difference. 'We really ought to disabuse the poor fellow, and make him aware that it is the difference between red and yellow, not blue and green, that he has learned'. This would be reasonable enough to say about him. It is one thing to insist a person can know that P despite his refusal or inability to avow this knowledge. It is another to say he is aware of knowing that P in the face of his refusal or inability, or even of his forcible *dis*avowal. To insist on the former may have some plausibility. To insist on the latter seems perverse.

'He is aware that he knows that P' cannot, then, be equivalent to 'He is aware that he is in a state apt for.... etc...'. Similar arguments could show that 'He is not aware that he knows that P' cannot be equivalent to 'He is not aware that he is in a state apt. . . .etc. . . '. Hence the 'functional' doctrine does not allow us to draw a distinction — at any rate, not in the right place — between 'conscious' and 'unconscious' knowledge or belief.

I do not place too much reliance on the above argument, since I am not too certain that the objectionable equivalences are necessary consequences of the 'functional' doctrine. Certainly they seem to be, as the doctrine is usually stated. As we saw, given the definition of (a) 'He knows that P' as (b) 'He is in a state apt. . . .etc. . . ', then substitution of (b) for (a) in (c) 'He is aware that he knows that P' yields (d) 'He is aware that he is a state apt. . . .etc. . .'. But, I have argued, (c) and (d) cannot be equivalent; hence (b) cannot be an acceptable definition of (a). Perhaps, though, the 'functional' doctrine could be stated differently, so that the equivalence of (c) and (d) is not forced upon it. But, as things stand, we have not been offered a reasonable way of drawing the distinction, crucial to the doctrine, between 'conscious', 'explicit' knowledge or belief, and 'unconscious', 'implicit', 'tacit', knowledge or belief.

2. I now turn to an objection against the grammatical knowledge postulated by KLT, through the 'functional' doctrine, that I will call 'Nagel's argument'. For it is to be found fairly clearly stated by Nagel in his article 'Linguistics and Epistemology'. His presentation, though, does suffer from a certain opacity as to the significance of the point argued, and perhaps from an actual misconception of what is being shown. I will try to make good these shortcomings. But, first, let me quote at some length from Nagel:

Under what conditions can knowledge of a language

governed by certain rules be described as knowledge of those rules? It will be instructive in this connection to consider another type of knowledge that cannot be explicitly formulated by its possessor, namely unconscious knowledge in the ordinary psychoanalytic sense. . . . The psychoanalytic ascription of unconscious knowledge, . . . does not depend simply on the possibility of organizing the subject's responses and actions in conformity with the alleged unconscious material. In addition . . . it is usually possible to bring him by analytical techniques to *see* that the statement in question expresses something that he knows or feels. That is, he is able eventually to acknowledge the statement as an expression of his own belief, if it is presented to him clearly enough and in the right circumstances. Thus what was unconscious can be brought, at least partly, to consciousness. It is essential that his acknowledgement *not* be based merely on the observation of his own responses and behaviour, and that he comes to recognize the rightness of the attribution from the inside.

. . . So long as it would be possible with effort to bring the speaker to a genuine recognition of a grammatical rule as an expression of his understanding of the language, rather than to a mere belief, based on the observation of cases, that the rule in fact describes his competence, it is not improper I think to ascribe knowledge of that rule to the speaker. It is not improper, even though he may never be presented with a formulation of the rule and consequently may never come to recognize it consciously.

. . . But when we consider the alleged innate contribution to language-learning . . . there is reason to doubt that the principles of such a linguistic acquisition device, when they have been formulated, could evoke internal recognition from individuals who have operated in accordance with them. . . . It seems not to be required even (by Chomsky and others) that such internal recognition should *ever* be available or possible, no matter how much effort is expended on it (pp. 175-7).

As we see from the third paragraph, Nagel restricts the point he is making to the principles, rules, categories, etc. of a universal, allegedly innate, grammar. But this seems to be an unnecessary restriction. For, typically, the rules of English grammar in particular are sufficiently complex and abstract to elicit no recognition 'from the inside' when formulated. Who, for example, would recognize the following rules, without retrospective observation of his past behaviour, as an expression of what he has always been doing, even after the symbols have been translated for him, and even if he could understand them:

(56) (a) *That-Insertion* (optional)
$_{NP}[NP\ S] \rightarrow _{NP}[NP\ that\ S]$.
where $S \neq _{S}[_{NP}[X\ Prep\ Y]\ Z]$

(b) *WH-Attachment* (obligatory)
$_{NP}[NP_1\ _{S}[_{NP}[X\ NP_1\ Y]\ Z]] \rightarrow$
$_{NP}[NP_1\ _{S}[_{NP}[X_{NP}[\begin{smallmatrix}WH\\NP_1\end{smallmatrix}\ NP_1]\ Y]\ Z]]$.

(Sanders and Tai : p. 190).

Nagel's point, then, is this. A condition for extending terms like 'knowledge' and 'belief' beyond the uncontroversial paradigms is that the persons in question can be brought to recognize or acknowledge certain descriptions of their behaviour simply as a result of having these presented to them, and not on the basis of an observational study of their behaviour to see if it matches the proferred descriptions. 'Ah, yes. Now I can see that this is what I have been doing all along', must be the typical reaction. Since statements of the rules, structures, etc. of a generative grammar typically elicit no such reaction, the condition for attributing knowledge of these rules or structures is missing.

We have here, perhaps, not so much an argument against the 'functional' doctrine as an alternative proposal for extending our talk of knowledge and belief — a proposal, I would urge, with the greater intuitive plausibility. For one thing, if we do not insist on Nagel's condition, it is difficult to see how, within psychoanalysis, unconscious knowledge or motives could be distinguished from mere causes of behaviour. It is noticeable, too, that even proponents of the 'functional' doctrine produce examples in favour of their doctrine which gain plausibility from meeting with Nagel's condition. Armstrong, for instance, gives as an example of unconscious knowledge the case of a person who, on being told the solution to a problem, immediately reacts by saying he knew it all along. He does not have to look back at his past behaviour to see that he has been acting in accordance with what he is said to know.

Certainly we must distinguish between the person who, on having a rule cited to him, immediately recognizes it as a true description of his behaviour, and the person who can do no such thing but who, so to speak, must take the part of an outside observer to check that his past behaviour has accorded with the rule. It seems plausible to extend terms like 'know the rule' in the first sort of case only.

But why is it plausible? How do we justify the feeling that only where there is Nagel's 'recognition', and not merely a functionally equivalent state, do we have a case of knowledge or belief? Nagel himself does not try to answer these questions, but I suspect a wrong answer to them lurks in the passages quoted. Certainly there is a wrong answer to give, which would run something like this:

> When we judge that a person knows or believes something, we are inferring that he is in a certain state. Explicit avowals, or professions of belief, provide near-conclusive evidence that he is in such a state. *Ex hypothesi,* this evidence is lacking in the controversial cases. Merely for the person to behave in the general ways that a person who uncontroversially knows or believes might behave would provide much too weak evidence for supposing him to be in the same state as the other person. We need more evidence than that. The extra evidence is provided by the readiness with which a person sometimes acknowledges and recognizes a description of his behaviour 'from the inside'. While this is not conclusive evidence, it is fairly reliable evidence from which to infer that a person is in the same state as one who uncontroversially knows or believes.

By this answer, then, our intuitive feeling about the need for the 'acknowledgeability' condition is explained by the fact that this provides good evidence, necessary in addition to other behavioural evidence, for inferring that persons know in just the way, explicit avowal apart, that people in the uncontroversial cases do. I suspect, perhaps wrongly, that some such view might underlie Nagel's own presentation. He writes, for example, that when we get a person to acknowledge 'from the inside' then 'what was unconscious . . . (is) . . . brought, at least partly, to consciousness'. This could suggest that what relates the controversial to the paradigmatic case of knowledge is some common state, at first unconscious, to which we can infer on the basis of the subsequent act of acknowledgement.

I will not spell out in any detail why I find the above view of the import of recognition and acknowledgement unsatisfactory. My reasons would closely parallel those levelled, in the last chapter, against the view that rule-following behaviour serves as evidence for rule-following. They are reasons which Wittgenstein, Ryle, and others have presented in some detail against a certain picture of the relation between behaviour, (especially avowal and the readiness to avow), and epistemic descriptions. Let me say just this: suppose a person acknowledged a rule 'from the inside' in Nagel's way, on what grounds could we then doubt that he knew the rule all along? Only, I think, by either supposing that he is lying in acknowledging the rule, or on the general conceptual ground that such readiness to acknowledge does not really justify extension of our attributions of knowledge. In neither case do we have insufficient evidence, and nor is it clear what could be meant by saying our evidence was insufficient.

A better answer to the question of how we might justify our feeling that Nagel's condition must be met if we are to speak of knowledge and belief — one which, if satisfactory is less problematical than the other view — might run as follows: To justify extension of terms like 'knowledge' and 'belief' beyond the paradigms, there must be sufficient analogy between the extended cases and the paradigms. There is a fairly smooth progression from being able, here and now, to avow knowledge of some rule R, through being unable to do so only because one has momentarily forgotten the rule, to the case of being ready to acknowledge 'R', once it is formulated for the person, as a description of a rule with which one's behaviour has accorded. Just as a person who knows from memory that he was in Paris — even if his memory needs jogging — does not require further evidence to make his claim that he was there, so sometimes a person can be brought to recognize that certain descriptions fit their behaviour without requiring retrospective evidence that this has been so. In both cases, it is reasonable to say the person knew something — before either the jogging of his memory, or the formulation of a description for him. Merely behaving in a way that a person who paradigmatically knows the rule might behave provides too tenuous a link with the paradigms to warrant extension of the relevant terms. For there are cases where people do behave like this, but where we should surely not want to attribute to them the knowledge or beliefs in question. The baby who buries his toys behaves like a person who believes that buried things are less likely to be lost. But there is no good reason to suppose the baby believes this. For all that his experience of the world has shown him, there might be subterranean creatures far more likely to steal his buried toys than we daylight creatures are to take the ones on the playroom floor. If the baby could be got to acknowledge the principle of 'burying makes safe', things would be different; but he can not, so they are not. I suppose the 'functionalist' might agree that our baby does not have the relevant belief, but deny that this has anything to do with the inapplicability of Nagel's condition. He might say that it is a case where explanations in terms of beliefs or knowledge are just not appropriate. But why are they not? He cannot say the be-haviour in question is not of a type which is *sometimes* explained in such terms. I, for one, bury my toys or my pieces of eight because I believe that burying makes safer. The behaviour is not like the 'behaviour' of the digestive system, which indeed does not lend itself to epistemic explanation. If the behaviour of the baby is not appropriately explained by reference to his knowledge or beliefs this can only be, as far as I can see, because the baby does nothing sufficiently analogous to what paradigm possessors of knowledge do. None of this is to say that readiness to acknowledge 'from the inside' is evidence for just the same thing that actual avowal is evidence for. Avowal is a criterion for paradigmatic ascriptions of knowledge and belief. Readiness to acknowledge 'from the inside' is a criterion for ascribing knowledge and beliefs in other cases. And there should be no temptation to think that the paradigm and extended cases are identical except for the alleged evidential symptoms. The difference between an item of conscious and unconscious knowledge is not like that between the table in front of the curtain and the table behind it. There is not a single state of knowing that is veiled from, or open to the gaze of, the knower. Rather, an item of knowledge is unconscious when there is something that he cannot, here and now, avow but which, under certain eliciting conditions, he can be brought to recognize without retrospective evidence of his past behaviour. And it is appropriate to describe the person as having known something because of the intelligible links between his case and the paradigmatic or nearly paradigmatic ones.

I am not sure if the above view does make out a strong case for extending our epistemic descriptions to cases which meet Nagel's condition. I am more sure, and more concerned, that no stronger view is acceptable — no view, that is, according to which we can extend those descriptions to cases which do not even meet that condition. At any rate, it is clear that, by this condition, fluent speakers do not have knowledge of more than a scrap of their generative grammars.

3. The strongest objection, I think, to the 'functional' doctrine, and to any claim that ordinary speakers have knowledge of a generative grammar, has close affinities to the argument of p. 53ff against the objectionable 'process/act' view of rule-following$_2$.

Throughout his writings, Quine has insisted upon the crucial connection between existence and identity conditions. 'No existence without identity' might be the slogan. Applied to our area of concern, the point will be that no states of knowledge or belief can be postulated unless there are identity conditions for them. If there is no way of telling what a person knows or believes, then no knowledge or belief should be attributed to him.

The 'functional' doctrine, unfortunately, fails to provide identity conditions for the states of belief and knowledge postulated. For, despite claims to the contrary, the behaviour which allegedly results from such states cannot serve to identify them, to distinguish one from another. Certainly 'functionalists' are well aware of the importance of identifying the states. Thus Fodor's insistence that

> the hypothesized psychological constructs are individuated primarily or solely by reference to their alleged causal consequences (1968b : p. 108).

But this could only be true, if true at all, if 'behaviour' or 'causal consequences' include avowals and expressions of knowledge or belief, or the sort of 'acknowledgement' behaviour recently discussed. Behaviour and consequences of these kinds, however, are precisely what 'functionalists' cannot have in mind, since they are not to be found among typical, fluent speakers of a language.

In the last chapter we saw that any rule-following behaviour (RFB) which accords with some rule R also accords with rules R1 . . . Rn, where 'R'. . . . . .'Rn' are extensionally equivalent descriptions. This vitiated the attempt to explain RFB in terms of following$_2$ a rule since, as was not the case with rule-following$_1$, no sense could be lent to supposing that one rule rather than another was being followed$_2$. Equally, if we have nothing but RFB to go by (and the 'functionalist' admits we do not), then there can be no reason to attribute to a person the belief that R is a rule of his grammar, rather than the belief that R1, or R2, . . . or Rn is a rule. Any one of these beliefs would have the same consequences as any other. Or, to get away from rules for a moment, attributing to a speaker the belief that A and B are categories of his grammar will have indistinguishable consequences from attributing to him the belief that C and D are categories of his grammar, where A and B are proposed on one theory and include just the strings that C and D, proposed on an alternative theory, include.

Some examples might help[1]. Suppose that one grammar contains the two following rewrite rules

1 X → Y
2 Z → Y

while an alternative grammar contains the single, collapsed rule

$$3\begin{Bmatrix} X \\ Z \end{Bmatrix} \to Y$$

Now anyone whose speech accords with rules 1. and 2. will automatically be speaking in accordance with rule 3. as well; and it will make no difference whether we ascribe to him the belief that 1. and 2. are rules of his grammar, or the belief that 3. is a rule of his grammar. The question 'Which does he really believe?' could have no answer in terms of the only kinds of behaviour that can be admitted as relevant on the 'functional' doctrine. This is not to say, incidentally, that there will be no consequences for the grammarian in preferring 1. and 2. to 3. or vice-versa. The choice is not arbitrary. Suppose the language alters, so that while sentences are still produced in accordance with 1. they are no longer produced in accordance with 2.. In that case it will be convenient to have a grammar for the language, prior to the change, which contains the separate rules 1. and 2. rather than the collapsed rule 3.. For then the linguistic change in question can be portrayed as consisting, simply, of the dropping out of a single rule (2.). Otherwise it would have to be portrayed as the dropping out of the rule (3.) and the introduction of a new one (1.).[2] But a consideration like this has no bearing on the question of which rule(s) the speaker really believes his language to obey.

Again, suppose that certain strings containing the constituents *a*, *b*, and *c* are analysed by one grammar into the labelled bracketing ((*ab*)*c*), and by a rival grammar into (*a*(*bc*)). Speakers who produce, understand, and judge such sentences

74

to be well-formed could just as well be said to believe that their structure is $((ab)c)$ as to believe it is $(a(bc))$. It is true that speakers may sometimes feel a tendency to group the constituents in one way rather than another. But, in the first place, this test is by no means always available; either no natural pull is felt, or different people feel different pulls. More important, it is quite unclear what the significance of any such feelings might be. (See the following chapter). Certainly feelings as to how constituents might naturally be grouped are not always to be taken seriously. This is presupposed when deep structures are postulated whose bracketings differ from the surface bracketings speakers naturally provide. For example, the fact that speakers might naturally feel like providing the following bracketing

(Hunting lions) (can be dangerous)

does not deter the grammarian from insisting that 'hunting lions' is not a genuine constituent, on at least one interpretation of the sentence.

'Grammar', as Stich says, 'is afflicted with an embarrassment of riches' (1972 : p. 807). There are indefinitely many sets of rules, structures, or categories which can be used to describe or generate the sentences of a language. Attributing to a speaker the belief that one rule or category belongs to his grammar will not have behavioural consequences, of an admissible type, which differ from those of attributing to him a quite different belief. Hence these behavioural consequences do not allow us to identify what beliefs, or what knowledge, speakers have. Hence, by the condition laid down earlier, no beliefs or knowledge should be attributed to speakers at all. Insistence to the contrary will have embarrassing results. First, it will never be possible to tell if two speakers share the same beliefs about their language. And if that is so, talk of *the* grammatical beliefs of a speech community becomes absurd. Second, when coupled with the claim that selection of a grammar must be based on what the speaker has actually 'internalized', it would mean there could be no reason at all for preferring one extensionally equivalent grammar to another. Other embarrassing consequences will emerge in a moment.

I neither know, nor particularly care, if it is actually senseless to postulate beliefs and knowledge which fail criteria for identity. But certainly the impossibility of answering questions like 'When do two speakers have the same beliefs?' or 'Does the speaker believe the same today as yesterday?' would suggest that, in a good sense, we just do not know what we are talking about in postulating such beliefs. It is useless to say that they are beliefs which are just like paradigm, uncontroversial beliefs, differing only in respect of avowability or acknowledgeability. The reply to that will be like the one Wittgenstein gave to the man who could see no difficulty in telling the time on the sun. Nor is it any use suggesting either (a) the speaker does in fact believe that only certain categories belong to his grammar; it is just that *we* cannot tell which ones, or (b) he believes that *all* extensionally equivalent categories describe his language. The reply to the first suggestion is that our inability to identify the speakers' beliefs or knowledge is not due to any contingent limitations on our powers of investigation. A witness to a murder, totally paralysed by the shock, will forever prevent us from discovering whom he believes the murderer to be. But we would not, for that reason, deny he has such a belief. But in the case of fluent speakers, there is nothing analogous to our witness' paralysis which prevents us from identifying their beliefs, and nothing analogous to his cure from paralysis that will make it possible to identify their beliefs. Hence we face the morbid consequences mentioned in the previous paragraph.

The effect of the second suggestion is to drive a huge wedge between the nature of the knowledge and belief being postulated and knowledge or belief of the uncontroversial, or intelligibly extended, type. Thus it is tantamount to admission that speakers have no grammatical knowledge or belief in any respectable senses of those terms. For, ordinarily, 'know' and 'believe' are *intensional* terms. From the fact that A knows that P, we cannot infer he knows that P', where P and P' are extensionally equivalent. I know my wife is my wife, but I do not know that she is the great-great-grandmother of the man who will eat strawberries in a space capsule on June 18 2100 A.D., even though 'my wife' and 'the great-great-grandmother . . . ' have the same extension. (This is not to deny that epistemic terms can be given extensional interpretations, but for this to be natural, a special setting is required.[3] Anyway, the other intensional interpretation is always available). Equally, one could not ordinarily infer from the fact that a person knows C to be a category of his grammar that he knows C' to be one too, where C and C' are extensionally equivalent. That this could be inferred would be the consequence of the suggestion that a speaker knows all those categories or rules which are extensionally equivalent to any one that he knows. Such a consequence conflicts head-on with a central feature of epistemic terms — indeed, *the* feature that makes them epistemic terms. Hence it is unclear that what is postulated by KLT could be knowledge or belief except in purely stipulated senses of the words.

I conclude that the failure of the 'functional' doctrine to intelligibly justify the extension of 'knowledge' and 'belief' into the disputed areas, taken with earlier objections, demonstrates the bankrupcy of KLT.

I said earlier that there was a subsidiary issue to be looked at in this chapter concerning knowledge in particular, in contrast to mere belief, presumption, or whatever. The issue is of some importance, and subsidiary only in the sense that it is less directly related to our examination of KLT than others.

The earlier discussion is not meant to suggest that speakers do not have all sorts of beliefs about their language, of a quite humdrum and uncontroversial type. The beliefs I have in mind are *not* those concerning the abstract rules or categories of a generative grammar, but such beliefs as that (a) one word means the same as another, (b) a certain word is only used properly if certain conditions hold (e.g. that 'voluntary' and 'involuntary' can only qualify an action reckoned to be 'fishy' in some way), or (c) it is ungrammatical to use certain words in certain strings (e.g. that 'whom' in 'The dog whom I saw was barking' is ungrammatical). The question is 'Can such beliefs (assuming they are true) count as items of knowledge?'. Well, suppose we begin with some version of the claim that knowledge is justified true belief. The controversy is then going to revolve around whether the 'justification' clause is satisfied. Two broadly divergent views can be found in the literature, two opposed answers to our question. The first stream of thought, which I will dub the 'verificatory' view, runs somewhat as follows:

> A person who claims to know some fact about his language is not making a claim about his own speech habits alone, but about the publicly shared language that he and many others speak. His belief may be true, but how, unless he has conducted a respectable empirical survey of others' speech, or is apprised on good authority of the results of such a survey, can he be justified in his belief? And if he cannot, then his belief cannot count as a piece of knowledge. Granted his membership of a speech community gives him some reason to suppose that others speak as he does — but this does not provide him with the respectable, conclusive evidence which alone could justify his claim to know the facts about the language.[4]

The other stream of thought, which I will call the 'participatory' view, consists primarily in a rebuttal of the previous one, and might go as follows:

> It is just not true that a man's claim to knowledge is justified only if he has engaged in, or is at least apprised of, empirical verification of his beliefs and presumptions. A person may be justified in his beliefs simply through being a participant in a practice. The foreigner in the United States would have to test his beliefs about the rules of baseball by observation of games or consulting of rule-books. But the participant — the baseball player, or the spectator weaned on the game — requires no such justification. To accuse a participant of not knowing the rules of a practice is in effect to deny that he is a genuine participant. It is to treat him as a mere observer of the practice. Now the language-user is a participant *par excellence,* and it would be to misunderstand participation, and the justification it provides, to deny that he has knowledge about his language on the grounds that he has done no first- or second-hand verification.[5]

Doubtless a dialectic between supporters of these two views could be continued in a number of directions. The supporter of the 'verificatory' view might point to examples where native speakers are at odds in their beliefs, where someone therefore is clearly mistaken despite his being a participant.[6] The reply to this, no doubt, would be that while some speakers can be wrong some of the time, it does not follow that they could always be wrong or that some of their beliefs do not count as knowledge. Anyway, when speakers are mistaken, it is not, as the 'verificatory' view would have us think, 'due to over-hasty generalization from insufficient empirical data concerning the verbal behaviour of groups' (Searle 1969 : p. 14). There could be discussion, too, about the relevance or otherwise of examples like the baseball one.

Both views, I think, contain elements of truth, and a little later I shall try to sketch what these are. For the moment I am interested in looking at what would be a most unsuccessful way of fusing the two views. I am interested in doing this because we find just such a fusion attempted, I suspect, in KLT. Admittedly proponents of that thesis are concerned with more exotic 'beliefs' and 'knowledge' than the humdrum kinds mentioned on p. 77 with which our 'verificatory' and 'participatory' views are dealing. But the peculiar account of knowledge found in KLT might, I think, owe to dim discernment of the respective merits of these views.

KLT, by attributing knowledge to fluent speakers, sides to that extent with the 'participatory' view. But now consider the following passages:

> According to Chomsky's conception, the child formulates hypotheses about the rules of the linguistic description of the language whose sentences he is hearing, derives predictions from such hypotheses . . . , checks these predictions against the new sentences he encounters, (and) eliminates those hypotheses that are contrary to the evidence. . . . This process of hypothesis construction, verification, and evaluation repeats itself until the child matures past the point where the language acquisition device operates (Katz 1966 : p. 275).

> The child who learns a language has in some sense constructed the grammar for himself on the basis of his observation of sentences and nonsentences . . . (through a) data-handling or "hypothesis-formulating" ability of unknown character and complexity (Chomsky 1964 : p. 577).

Consider, too, the point frequently stressed by Chomsky and his followers that 'grammar' is used in a purposely ambiguous way, to refer both to the theory produced and tested by linguists and to the system 'internalized' by fluent speakers. The picture emerging is that what the fluent speaker does, or has done as a child, is closely analogous to what the empirical linguist does. He sets up hypotheses about features of his language; he tests these against his observations of the speech community; he selects those which stand up to the tests and which recommend themselves on such grounds as simplicity. In other words, the speaker does just the sort of thing that, according to the 'verificatory' view, must be done by a person if his claims to knowledge about his language are to be warranted. The speaker's beliefs and presumptions about his language are justified precisely because he has in fact verified them in a respectably scientific manner. Only, of course, the speaker unlike the linguist is not aware of formulating his hypotheses. And his testing of hypotheses occurs so quickly, or so privately, that not even he is aware of what he is doing. The data-processing in which he engages is not a type which we or he can ever observe in the way we can that of the girl at the computer centre. And the simplicity principle he employs in arriving at his beliefs is one which he would, no doubt, be surprised to find he had been employing.

I shall not take time off to criticize this view, or the picture of the baby scientists, juvenile masters of Popperian methodology, which figures in it. The nature of my criticisms could quickly be inferred from those directed against KLT in this and the previous chapters. I want only to stress the roots from which this picture grows. The roots are buried, partly, in the conviction shared with the 'participatory' view that speakers do have knowledge about their language, despite the fact that they have not, in any obvious way, set about verifying their beliefs. And they are buried, partly, in the conviction shared by the 'verificatory' view that only verification, at first— or second-hand, justifies a person's claim to know something. Join the roots together, and you have the conclusion that while speakers must have engaged in verification (since they do have knowledge), they must have engaged in it in esoteric, unobvious, private ways — so private as to be concealed from the speakers themselves. From the standpoint of this conclusion, both the 'verificatory' and 'participatory' views are seen to rest upon a mistaken assumption — the assumption that speakers have not engaged in verification. Both have ignored the baby scientist.

There is, I hope, a less bizarre way of reconciling the two views. (And now I am returning to views about such humdrum beliefs as that one word means the same as another). My remarks are brief, since they are to some degree incidental to the main theme of this essay.

Speakers do, I think, know various humdrum truths about their language. It would take a lot to convince me that I do not know that 'bachelor' and 'unmarried man' are synonymous in English, despite my never having carried out an empirical survey. But it does not follow that the stress on verificatory procedures is out of place when it comes to justifying the view that such beliefs count as knowledge. It is only because such beliefs could be confirmed according to standard canons of scientific enquiry that they can count as items of knowledge. This is not to say, simply, that they must be true. There is a school of thought in sociology, anthropology, and perhaps in linguistics, according to which *only* the participant can have knowledge about, or understanding of, the practices he engages in. The true beliefs of the participant, while they are items of knowledge, are not ones which can be confirmed by the verificatory techniques of the outside observer. This smacks too much of *Verstehen* and all its attendant problems of validation for me. Beliefs which *only* the participant is in a position to assess, even in principle, could not count as knowledge — nor, perhaps, as beliefs either. Again, if we stress the role of verification, we are not going to accept the view that some of the participant's beliefs about the practices he engages in are so 'clear and distinct', so self-validating, that they must count as knowledge irrespective of the possibility of confirming them in standard empirical ways.

None of this is to say that the given participant must have confirmed his beliefs in standard, verificatory ways if he is to be credited with knowledge. So it would seem, so far, that we are siding more heavily with the 'participatory' view. However, that view is mistaken in supposing that a speaker's beliefs count as knowledge because they are justified by virtue of his being a participant. Lewis, for example, is wrong to think that questioning a person's justification for his beliefs is tanta-mount to denying that he is a genuine participant, but merely an observer. I do not think the participant's beliefs are justi-fied — which is not to say they are unjustified. The connection between being a participant and claims to knowledge is not that the first justifies the second. Of course, it is because one is a participant that one has the beliefs one does, and because one is a participant that the beliefs have been arrived at in the way they have. There are beliefs which would be naturally and relatively unreflectingly expressed by anyone trained as a participant in a practice. These beliefs are, as it were, the natural and shared responses of a community constituted by its common practices. Such beliefs, I suggest, count as know-ledge. They are not guesses, and even less are they arrived at by generalization from restricted data. Were they guesses, or hastily formed hypotheses, they would be like the beliefs of a rash and second-rate social observer which, even if true, could not count as knowledge. But they are, rather, the natural responses of men trained in and engaged in certain practices as part of their social life. So it is not that participation pro-vides justification for beliefs. Rather, participation results in men having certain beliefs, and it is because the beliefs have resulted in this way that the participants can, without having justification for their beliefs, be said to know.[7]

Notes to Chapter 4

1   The examples are, of necessity, somewhat dull. While we know, on the basis of the theory of axiomatization, that it it is possible

to construct radically different, but extensionally equivalent grammars, it is no easy task to actually construct them. If I were to take rules excitingly different from, say, Chomsky's, there would be controversy as to whether the two sets really were equivalent.

2 See Kiparsky on the relation between linguistic change and criteria for grammars.

3 See my *Presupposition* for a detailed discussion of this point.

4 The 'verificatory' view has been held by Mates and Naess among others.

5 Some version or other of the 'participatory' view can be found in Cavell, Searle (1969), and Lewis. The baseball example is Searle's, and the point about questioning a participant's knowledge being a challenge to his genuine status as a participant, is Lewis'.

6 Mates does just this when he shows how Ryle and Austin are at odds over the ordinary uses of 'voluntary' and 'involuntary'.

7 I suspect the Wittgenstein of the *Philosophical Investigations* (though not, perhaps, of *On Certainty*) might endorse the point being made. As a result of being trained within a common form of life, men come to agree in the judgments they make (e.g. the judgment that *this* is how the rule should be applied at this point). Often they do not, and cannot, justify their claims to know what they judge to be the case, but it does not follow that they do not know.

Chapter 5

Linguistic Intuitions

In stark contrast to 'Bloomfieldian' writings, those of Chomsky and his followers are shot through with references to speakers' psychology, and especially with talk about their so-called 'intuitions'. Bloomfield, for whom science, including linguistics, 'requires none of the mentalistic terms' (p. 12), focuses almost entirely upon the strings produced by speakers. Chomsky concentrates equally, perhaps more, upon the intuitions which speakers have about these strings. I want to ask several questions about intuitions. What are they? What roles do they play in current linguistic theory? What support do they lend to KLT? And why is this support in fact bogus?

Linguistic intuitions are not intuitions in several or perhaps any of the usual senses of that polyhedric word. They are not supposed, for example, to be 'intuitive' as opposed to 'reasoned' or 'considered'. On the contrary, the alleged intuition that 'John is eager to please' is radically different in structure from 'John is easy to please' will only emerge, it is said, after rational consideration of the various paraphrases that the one sentence, and not the other, permits. Nor are speakers' judgments meant to be self-evident on immediate inspection. Chomsky stresses that the intuitive judgment that 'I had a book stolen' is triply ambiguous might require some effort to elicit. Some speakers may not be able to see it at all. Nor, of course, are these judgments intuitive in any philosophically weighty sense like Moore's or Prichard's. It is not being suggested that what speakers intuit are simple, unanalysable properties of sentences. On the contrary, the

84

intuition that a sentence is ambiguous concerns a complex set of rules, relations, and structures.

It is difficult in fact to see what can be meant by 'intuition' except the judgments that most fluent speakers, by virtue of being fluent, do or can make under suitable eliciting conditions. They are to be contrasted with those judgments about the language which only the professional linguist, on the basis of empirical research, is in a position to make — such as that the language belongs to the Indo-European family, or that a given word has altered meaning since 1500. Perhaps, therefore, the choice of the word is not a particularly happy one; though I shall suggest that, by at least one account of what speakers' intuitions are like, the word is not altogether inappropriate. For the moment, though, intuitions may be thought of as certain judgments which fluent speakers can make about the sentences of their language.

What, then, would be a representative list of intuitions? Linguists, unfortunately, differ on how intuitions are to be specified. The main trouble is that the specifications or descriptions given range from the relatively uncontroversial to the highly controversial and theory-laden. On the one hand — relatively uncontroversially — we are told that speakers can judge that certain sentences are well-formed, that some are ambiguous, or that some are closely related to others. On the other hand — this time, controversially — we are told they can judge that certain sentences accord with the rules of generative grammar, or that some sentences have two under-lying structures, or that some sentences have only superficial similarity in surface structure. Lyons writes:

> . . . for Chomsky the 'intuitions' of the speaker (that is to say, his mental representation of the grammar of his language) . . . are the true objects of description (p. 87).

If Lyons is right then not only does Chomsky identify intuitions with something whose status is highly dubious (i.e. the 'mental representation' of grammar), but the proper descriptions of them would have to be couched in the theoretical language of a generative grammar — since the main aim of such a grammar is to describe these intuitions.

We will return to these controversial, theory-laden descriptions of intuitions later. For the moment we might rest content with the following examples of intuitions — examples which frequently figure in the literature, and which do not, in any obvious way, beg disputable questions: Speakers can judge

(a) certain strings are well-formed, and others are ill-formed.
(b) certain sentences are ambiguous, though no single word occurring within them is ambiguous (e.g. 'I had the book stolen' or 'Flying planes can be dangerous').
(c) certain sentences are synonymous (e.g. 'The president made the decisions' and 'The decisions were made by the president').
(d) certain sentences are 'closely related' (e.g. 'He hit me' and 'Did he hit me?').
(e) certain sentences are 'very different', despite apparent close similarities between them (e.g. 'John is eager to please' and 'John is easy to please').

Let us grant that most fluent speakers can be got to make judgments like these under suitable eliciting conditions.

Linguistic intuitions have come to play major roles in linguistic theory — both in setting goals for grammars, and in providing tests of adequacy. Some of the roles to be mentioned have, it would seem, revolutionized the idea of what a grammar ought to be. First, it will be intuitions of type (a) that will serve to define 'grammaticality', to provide the strings that it is the job of a grammar to generate. For, as we saw in chapter 1, grammatical sentences cannot be equated with those that people actually do, with some frequency, produce. Nor can they simply be identified with those that people 'accept' without complaint or 'bizarreness reactions'. For many acceptable sentences are ungrammatical and many unacceptable ones (very, very long sentences, for example) are grammatical. Clearly, therefore, we must be able to elicit from speakers judgments about well-formedness, if we are to be able to reject acceptable sentences as nevertheless ungrammatical. Once we have become theoretical, of course, we can define 'grammaticality' in terms of the rules of our theory. But the initial choice of rules must be guided by appeal to speakers' judgments.

Second, as we have also seen, various grammars could succeed in generating all and only well-formed sentences of the language. But, it is argued, it would not follow that one grammar is as good as the next. Chomsky's basic charge against phrase structure grammars was not that they fail in their generative capacity, but that they do not 'adequately represent' sentences so as to 'accord with' or 'correspond to' intuitions like (b) to (e). He writes

> . . . the structural descriptions assigned to sentences by the grammar . . . must, for descriptive adequacy, correspond to the linguistic intuitions of the native speaker, in a substantial and significant class of cases (1965 : p. 24)[1]

A phrase structure grammar fails, for example, by having to provide just two quite separate phrase markers for the sentences 'He hit me' and 'Did he hit me?', since this does not 'reveal' the relation between the sentences that people intuit. So, then, intuitions play a role in determining the so-called 'descriptive adequacy' of a grammar.

Finally, intuitions pose for the linguist not merely the problem of drawing up a grammar that 'reveals' sentences in accordance with them, but also the problem of producing a grammar which will explain how speakers have come to have these intuitions. Two grammars may be equally 'revealing', and therefore of equal descriptive adequacy, but only the one which is consistent with an acquisition model, explaining how speakers come to know language in the way they do, will have 'explanatory adequacy'. This means, in effect, that grammar must become a psychological theory. To some extent the whole of this book is a critique of this conception of grammar, but remarks specifically upon the goal of 'explanatory adequacy' will be found in chapter 9.

But in what way, precisely, could reflection upon linguistic intuitions lend support to KLT? Well, a number of answers have been suggested. But I will focus upon an argument which tries to forge a very direct link between intuitions and existence of knowledge of the kind proposed by KLT. It runs something like this:

> Descriptions (a) to (e) of intuitions are examples of just one kind of description that can be given of intuitions. Others are possible which make it clear that speakers' intuitions and judgments have, as their very content or subject-matter, features as specified by generative grammar. Intuitions, that is, are intuitions *about* deep structures, transformation rules, theoretical categories, and the like. Grammatical knowledge of the type proposed by KLT does not so much explain these intuitions and judgments as get itself revealed in them. Intuitions are, so to speak, instances of such knowledge in action. Just as a person could not judge that a given rule of chess has just been broken unless he knew the rules of chess, so a person could not judge that a sentence accords with certain rules unless he knew the grammar to which these rules belong.

Before assessing this argument, a word about the place of my remarks within the context of my critique of KLT. Obviously I cannot suppose that the argument stands any chance of establishing KLT, since I have already rejected it as an incoherent thesis. But it is worth pretending that I have not done this, or that I bungled it. Let us pretend, in other words, that there are no problems in referring to unconscious knowledge of grammar, or to rule-following of a type suitable for proponents of KLT. For I want to concentrate on the peculiarity of the argument just mentioned, not on the peculiarity of the thesis it is an argument for.[2]

This direct argument for KLT from the phenomena of linguistic intuition rests on the claim that a description or specification of an intuitive judgment should or could take the form

The speaker judges that. . . .

where the blanks are filled by a specification culled from generative grammatical theory. (Such descriptions are what I called 'controversial' on p. 85, in contrast to the 'uncontroversial' descriptions of types (a) to (e)). Examples will help make the claim clearer. Slobin discusses the intuition that the sentences 'The president makes the decisions' and 'The decisions are made by the president' are synonymous. He says this intuition is a judgment to the effect that 'the logical propositions underlying the active . . . and passive . . . above are identical, though the word order is changed' (p. 5). Chomsky, writing of a speaker's initial tendency to treat two dissimilar sentences as similar, says that at this stage 'it may not be in the least clear to (the) speaker . . . that the grammar that he has internalized in fact assigns very different syntactic analyses to the superficially analogous sentences . . . ' (1965 : p. 24). The implication, clearly, is that when the speaker comes to no longer regard the sentences as closely analogous, it *does* become clear to him that they have two quite distinct structural analyses. The point to note is that in both examples it is being held that a speaker can judge that . . . , where the blanks are filled by a theoretical description. In the one case he is said to judge that the logical propositions underlying sentences are identical; in the other that two sentences receive radically different structural analyses.

Now if intuitions were really like these, specifiable in such ways, then KLT would be established without further ado. For speakers could not make such judgments, with any understanding, unless they knew the grammar in terms of which their judgments are specified.

But why should it be thought that intuitions can be specified in these 'controversial' ways? Why, for example, should it be thought that a person judging two sentences to be closely related is thereby judging them to be related to a single underlying structure? One would suppose that this second judgment is made only by the sophisticated linguist. I fear that the reasoning, in so far as any is forthcoming, may simply be this: since, according to grammatical theory, pairs of 'closely related' sentences are identical with those having the same underlying structure, then the judgment that two sentences are 'closely related' is identical with the judgment that they have the same underlying structure.

Stated in this way, the reasoning is glaringly fallacious. 'A judged that . . . ' provides an 'opaque' context within which descriptions true of the same object or range of objects are not necessarily interchangeable *salva veritate*.[3] If I judge that the woman sitting over there is my wife, I am not *ipso facto* judging that she is the richest woman in the world, even though 'my wife' and 'the richest woman in the world' refer to the same person. I may, unfortunately, be quite unaware that this is so, and would certainly deny therefore that the woman over there is the richest in the world. It is notoriously difficult, of course, to say just what descriptions are interchangeable in opaque contexts, and why. Certainly, though, the permissibility of substitution must have something to do with what a person would assent to or avow. A starting suggestion would be: 'A judges that P' is true only if A would assent to or avow 'P'. But this would be too strong, for then all claims of the form 'This monolingual Frenchman judges that P', where 'P' is an English sentence, would be false. Our Frenchman, not understanding 'P', is unlikely to assent to, or dissent from, it. A refined suggestion would be: 'A judges that P' is true only if A would assent to 'P' or to something synonymous with it. And a weaker suggestion still would be that A must assent to 'P' or to something logically equivalent to it. I do not want to get embroiled in the general issue of opacity — and I do not need to. For it is obvious enough that some descriptions are not interchangeable within opaque contexts, and that the limit has been reached when the descriptions are only contingently satisfied by the same object(s) — as the example of my secretive, millionairess wife shows.

It might be replied, though, that the descriptions 'closely related sentences' and 'sentences with the same underlying structure' are not *contingently* satisfied by the same objects in the way 'my wife' and 'the richest woman in the world' are. Well, it can certainly be admitted that the respective identities are very different. Determining that the woman in the corner is my wife is not required for determining that she is the richest woman in the world. One could find out in one way that she is my wife, and in a quite independent way that she is the richest woman in the world. Presumably, though, determining that two sentences are 'closely related' is required for determining that they have the same underlying structure. That sentences are judged to be 'closely related' motivates that portion of the grammar which attributes the same underlying structure to them. The linguist does not ascertain that the sentences are judged in this way, and then, quite independently, discover them to have the same underlying structure.

I take it that the identity in question is what is sometimes called a 'theoretical identity' — and, to be sure, the status of theoretical identities is, in general, obscure. 'Genes are D.N.A. molecules', 'numbers are classes of classes', 'conscience is the superego', or "closely related' sentences are ones with the same underlying structure', are none of them easy to elucidate. And I do not want to attempt any general elucidation here. But I do want to say that, however we elucidate them, they do not warrant substitution of the relevant descriptions in opaque contexts; and that, even if this were not so in general, the identity which concerns us is not of the necessary kind that might, possibly, sustain substitution.

The best way, I think, of objecting to substitution of the relevant terms in opaque contexts is simply to draw attention to the highly peculiar consequences of doing the substitutions. It is clear to me that 'Johnny judged that $2 + 2 = 4$' is not replaceable by 'Johnny judged that the class of all classes with two members . . . etc . . . ' . The first sentence would describe a fairly normal child; the second makes him sound like a child prodigy. Again, one can not replace a sentence describing Mendel's judgments about the genes of green and yellow peas with a sentence describing his judgments about their D.N.A. structure. Mendel was pre-, and not post- Crick and Watson. To allow such replacements would be to attach to a person's powers of judgment knowledge of theoretical notions that emerge, perhaps, only centuries after his death. Other peculiar consequences will be mentioned later.

The particular identity that concerns us, moreover, is of a certain empirical type, and not of a necessary kind that could possibly support substitution in opaque contexts. To suppose it is of the latter type would be to confuse what is necessary with what can be known *a priori* — a confusion which Kripke has recently pinpointed with great force. It is true that we do not discover, by some additional piece of observation, that sentences judged to be 'closely related' are those with the same underlying structure. Rather, on the basis of some clear-cut cases of 'closely related' sentences, a theory has been erected which guarantees that these will have certain grammatical properties. Hence, one can infer from the fact that two sentences have the same underlying structure that they, or ones like them, are judged by speakers to be 'closely related'. But it does not follow that those sentences, which as a matter of fact, the grammar has assigned identical underlying structures to, had to be the ones which speakers judge to be 'closely related'. Of course, if they had not been judged in this way, the grammar would not have assigned to them the structures it has. But that does not alter the fact that sentences which *have been* assigned these structures might not have been ones speakers judged as 'closely related'. Once the reference of 'sentences with the same underlying structure' has been fixed, it is quite possible to imagine that the sentences referred to might not have had that characteristic (i.e. being judged as 'closely related') which motivated the grammatical description. Hence it is not a matter of necessity that sentences with the same underlying structure assigned them by the grammar should be those judged as 'closely related'. Hence if we were to allow that, in general, descriptions necessarily satisfied by the same objects are interchangeable in opaque contexts, that could not affect the present issue.[4]

It is open to the grammarian, naturally, to stipulate that what he *means* by 'ambiguous', 'grammatical', 'closely related', and so on, is stateable only in the terms of his theoretical apparatus. He could, for instance, stipulate that for him 'ambiguous' means 'having at least two underlying structures'. It might then follow that whoever judges a sentence to be ambiguous thereby judges it to have at least two underlying structures. But there is an obvious price to pay for this move. For it is no longer clear that speakers do make judgments about ambiguity (synonymy, grammaticality, relatedness, etc.) Whether or not they do will have become just as disputable as whether or not they can judge that . . . , where the blanks are filled by a theoretical specification. It is only in senses different from the stipulated ones that it is beyond dispute that speakers make judgments about ambiguity and the rest.

These objections to the 'controversial' way of specifying the content of intuitions do not, incidentally, depend upon denying that 'A judges that . . . ' *can* be interpreted transparently — in a manner, that is, which permits substitution of extensionally equivalent descriptions. A gloss for the transparent interpretation of 'A judges that S is ambiguous' might be 'A judges *of* the class of ambiguous sentences that it contains S'. Assuming that the class of ambiguous sentences is identical with the class of sentences having more than one underlying structure, then we may infer that A judges of this latter class that it contains S, and hence that, transparently interpreted, he judges that S has more than one underlying structure. But, in the first place, transparent readings cannot generally be normal or natural, and will, special context aside, be misleading.[5] It is alright to say 'Oedipus believed he wanted to make love to his mother' to someone acquainted with the legend. But to say this, rather than 'Oedipus believed he wanted to make love to Jocasta, who as a matter of fact happened to be his mother', will suggest to a person not acquainted with the legend that Oedipus was incestuously motivated, which of course he was not. That transparent readings could not generally be acceptable is shown by the following consideration: a person who judges that X is X would, if this is treated transparently, thereby be judging that every description is true of X which is, as it happens, true of X. His making the trivial judgment would entail his making every true judgment about X there is to make. What was trivial seems to have become superhuman. The argument is this: if the descriptions 'X', 'X1', . . . 'Xn' are all satisfied by X, then they are all interchangeable for one another within transparent contexts. So, if 'A judges that X is X' is treated transparently, then it is also the case that A judges that X is X1, X2, . . . Xn. Second, and following on from the previous consideration, judgments transparently treated exhibit nothing about a man's mind — about his intellect, his powers of judgment, his scope of knowledge, or whatever. As we have just seen, someone who judges that X is X thereby judges that everything true of X is true of X, on the transparent interpretation. But we cannot conclude that he is some kind of omniscient being. Indeed, we can conclude nothing whatever about his mental powers except that he knows a thing to be what it is. In the transparent sense of 'judge', everyone judges as true every description that is, as a matter of fact, true. And this is a *reductio ad absurdum* of the claim that transparent judgment could have any place in psychological description. So while we can treat 'A judges that S is ambiguous' in such a way as to infer 'A judges that S has more than one underlying structure', we do so at the expense of making descriptions of judgments alien to psychology. If linguists are concerned with such judgments, then linguistics is not the subfield of psychology that Chomsky insists it is.

There is a less direct, and marginally more hopeful, route a proponent of KLT might take towards treating intuitions as exhibitions of generative grammatical knowledge. For considerations are sometimes advanced which would make it at least excusable and to some degree natural to specify the content of intuitions in theoretical, 'controversial' terms. The considerations I have in mind run along these lines:

> When a speaker judges that two sentences are 'closely related', he is judging them to have *something* in common. The speaker, admittedly, is unable to judge what this is; that is the job of the professional linguist. Equally, when a speaker judges that two sentences mean the same, he is again judging them to have *something* in common – the proposition, say, which according to some linguists and philosophers, is denoted or expressed by both sentences. Now it could certainly be misleading to infer from 'A judges that S and S' have something in common' to 'A judges that S and S' are derived from a single underlying structure' or to 'A judges that S and S' denote the same proposition'. However, it is not entirely unnatural or misconceived to do so. For in judging that 'related' or synonymous sentences are those with items in common, the speaker is displaying his acquaintance with the objects that syntax and semantics goes on to describe and specify. His judgment, so to speak, invites specification in theoretical terms. The linguist's job is to describe what the speaker

knows only by acquaintance — the common item, for example, shared by the synonymous S and S'.

Before assessing this line of consideration, I want to expand on an earlier comment. I said (p. 85) that by a certain view of what speakers' linguistic judgments are like, the term 'intuitive' would not be an inappropriate one for describing them. The view I meant is the one just sketched. For consider the following, perfectly natural things a person might say:

> 'I just knew there was something wrong with him. I could not tell what it was. But my intuition turned out to be right. He had just lost his job', or
> 'My intuition told me there was something funny about the other guests in the hotel, though I could not put my finger on what it was. But, as you know, it turned out they were all members of the train-robbery gang'.

In other words, we often speak of a person's intuition where he knows or feels that something is the case, although he is unable to specify what it is, unable to 'put his finger on it'. *Somewhat* analogously, we might talk of a speaker's linguistic intuition if we regard this as displaying his acquaintance with something which, though specifiable, is not specifiable by him.

The consideration sketched involves a number of difficulties, some of which go right to the heart of transformational grammatical theory, quite apart from the psychological doctrines extracted from it. But let us begin with the proposed picture of speakers' intuitions. Certainly one can grant that speakers who judge sentences to be 'closely related' or synonymous are judging them to have something in common. But it is not clear that one need grant this except in the most bloodless sense of 'something in common'. In this bloodless sense, to judge that two sentences have something in common *is* to judge that they are 'closely related' or that they are synonymous. Now I see no reason to think that speakers judge sentences to have something in common in any more weighty sense. In particular, I see no reason to suppose that speakers judge there to be certain single objects — underlying structures, propositions, etc. — to which two sentences are related, and by virtue of which they are 'closely related' or synonymous. I, for one, would be rather puzzled if asked 'What does an indicative sentence have in common with its corresponding interrogative?'. For it seems to me that the questionner has answered his own question. The one sentence asks what the other states: *that is* how the two are related. Equally, having said that two sentences are synonymous, have I not already said what they have in common? They mean the same. I need not think — and would not think, unless I had read certain philosophers and linguists — that there is, in addition, some common item they have in common, by virtue of which they mean the same. An analogy might help here. In the bloodless sense, there is nothing wrong with saying that a veridical perception has something in common with an illusory perception that a person might mistake for the veridical one. But what is in common may be completely explained once it is said that the one perception is an illusory version of the other. We need not postulate that, in addition, there is some single object present in both perceptions. To postulate this would involve commitment to sense-data, and sense-data of the reified sort which most would be loathe to admit.[6]

The claim that speakers are acquainted, intuitively, with objects or items common to certain sentences is but a reflection, at the psychological level, of the transformational grammarian's view that 'relatedness' and synonymy are to be explained in terms of such objects or items. As we saw in Chapter 1, a frequently cited advantage of a transformational over a phrase structure grammar is precisely that the former does, while the latter does not, 'represent' or 'reveal' the common ingredients of 'closely related' or synonymous sentences.

> What we cannot represent within the framework of a phrase structure grammar . . . is the fact that . . . pairs of sentences like 'The man hit the ball' and 'The ball was hit by the man' are 'felt' by native speakers to be related, or to belong together in some way . . . (Lyons : p. 63).

For Katz, the provision of a single underlying structure for the sentences 'Invisible God created the visible world' and

'God who is invisible created the visible world' *reveals* and. provides a *natural explanation* of their synonymy. (1972 : p. 60). So, it is the common objects assigned to sentences by a transformational grammar which reveal and explain 'relatedness' and synonymy; and it is rudimentary, intuitive acquaintance with such objects which explains speakers' judgments on these matters. I have rejected the second of these claims. Let us examine the first.

The above argument for deep structure, exemplified by Lyons and Katz, involves, it seems to me, a kind of mimetic fallacy. Because — so the reasoning seems to run — 'related' or synonymous sentences have something in common, because they are similar in some respect, then any representation of the sentences (in the form, say, of labelled bracketings or trees) must contain or display the ingredient they have in common, the shared item by virtue of which they are similar. The representations must, as it were, mimic the sentences by having something in common, by containing similar or identical features. Only, in the case of the representations, all of this must be open to view, laid out for all to clearly see.

Now I have already argued that the bloodless sense in which *of course* 'related' sentences have something in common does not mean that there is some single ingredient that both share, and by virtue of which they are related. Hence there is no reason to think there is such an ingredient to be patently displayed in representations of the sentences. But, apart from this, the view in question involves a peculiarly stunted conception of how similarities between things ought to be represented or portrayed. I suppose that all paintings from a certain school are similar in various ways, and so, bloodlessly, have something in common. Are we to suppose that, hidden away in some Venetian attic, is *the* painting of the school, having for all to see just the features which are shared by all paintings from the school? Or, was there in the heads of the Venetian painters a single, abstract blueprint from which all the actual paintings were 'derived'? And must an art historian in analysing the similarities between paintings of the school provide a single, quintessential model to which they are all related? Obviously not. The best way to get a person to recognize the similarities between the paintings might be, simply, to line them up before him and get him to look.

The proponent of a phrase structure grammar, it seems to me, should be rightly puzzled by the charge that his phrase markers for, say, the sentences 'He hit me' and 'Did he hit me?' do not 'reveal', 'represent', or 'explain' the connection between them. Why has not one revealed the connection by simply writing them out? And does not one explain the connection by simply pointing out that one is the interrogative version of the other, that the one would answer what the other asks? It is not clear to me what further is 'revealed' or 'explained' by drawing up a diagram which displays a single figure to which both sentences can be connected.

It is difficult, at this stage, to avoid mention of the notorious John, with his eagerness and easiness. Chomsky's John seems destined to join that select band of philosophical exemplaries which already contains 'the third man', 'the present king of France', and 'N.N.'. It is said that a phrase structure grammar, by having to provide two similar looking phrase markers for the sentences 'John is eager to please' and 'John is easy to please', fails to 'reveal', 'represent', 'display', etc. the radical difference between them. This charge is just the reverse of the one mentioned in the previous paragraphs. And I find the same difficulty with it. Having described the importantly different ways in which the two sentences are paraphrased, I am not clear what is left to 'reveal' about the difference between them. I fail to see that provision of two dissimilar looking representations or diagrams should be the best, or only, way of doing this. To suppose that it is, is to fall once more for a mimetic fallacy. You might as well suppose that when reproducing two very different paintings in a book, they must be printed on different kinds of photographic paper.

I am not, incidentally, holding out a brief for phrase structure grammars over and against transformational ones. There may be considerable point in representing sentences in the latters' manner, and in distinguishing deep from surface structures. It may be, for example, that the simplest set of rules yet devised for generating well-formed sentences will contain rules of different types, in accordance with which more than one phrase marker will be provided for each sentence. But such a reason as this is quite unrelated to previous arguments mentioned. It does not require underlying phrase markers to 'reveal' sentences in accordance with speakers' intuitions, nor diagrammatic pictures of the objects or items common to certain sentences. Sentences which have something in common are not thereby related to a certain single object or item, nor do speakers have intuitions of a kind which the phrase markers of some grammar could mimic.

It might be felt that *surely* grammar has something to tell us about speakers' judgments and intuitions; that, surely, linguists have not been completely at sea in thinking their analyses bear upon our linguistic knowledge. Well, I do not want to go into this in any detail now. I reserve for the final chapter some general remarks on the psychological bearings of grammar. But I can say this much: of course there is a sense in which grammar tells us about speakers' intuitions and about what they know. People intuit and know that certain sentences are ambiguous, and the job of a grammar, *inter alia,* is to provide an account of ambiguity. If ambiguity (of a certain kind) is best treated in terms of alternative derivations from a single underlying structure, then we are being told something about ambiguity – and hence about an object of human knowledge. In the same way, set theory, by telling us about numbers, tells us something about the things people have knowledge of, since people have all kinds of knowledge about numbers. But just as set theory is not a psychological theory simply because it deals with objects encompassed in human knowledge, nor is grammar a psychological theory because it does the same. That a grammar tells us about objects (e.g. sentences) encompassed in knowledge does not mean it tells us of the thought processes men engage in, the concepts they employ, the mental acts they perform, or the rules they follow. More of this, as I said, in chapter 10.

I conclude, then, that no support for KLT can be found in the fact that speakers make judgments about, and do not simply produce and understand, utterances. Neither the brusquely direct route (p. 87 ff), nor the less direct route (p. 94 ff), led us to see in intuitions exhibitions of grammatical knowledge of the kind proposed by KLT. There are, no doubt, other routes that might be tried. But other arguments, I think would reduce to ones considered in earlier chapters, or at least be so similar to these as to warrant no separate treatment. For example, if making intuitive judgments is included in rule-following behaviour (RFB) — as indeed it was included in chapter 3 — then it will be argued that intuitions, like the rest of RFB, can only be explained as resulting from unconscious, non-trivial, grammatical knowledge of rules. This line of argument has, I hope, been discredited already.

Notes to Chapter 5

1 Postal, along the same lines, holds that 'structural descriptions must provide an account of all the grammatical information which is in principle available to the native speaker' (p. 137).

2 I suppose, too, there is always the chance that if anything could be made of the argument we might be tempted to review our earlier dismissals of the conclusion.

3 The terms 'opaque' and 'transparent' (see pp. 92 ff) are Quine's. In employing them, and defining them in terms of substitutability, I am not committing myself to various things Quine has to say about opacity and transparency, such as that no quantification into opaque contexts is ever permissible, or that expressions occurring in opaque contexts never do so referentially.

4 To take an analogy — and this is Kripke's own example — having fixed the reference of 'one metre in length' as anything equal in length to the standard bar in Paris, one can then imagine of anything encompassed in this reference, *including* the standard bar itself, that it might not have been one metre in length. It can be known *a priori* that the standard bar is one metre in length, but it is quite imaginable that this bar should not have been the length it in fact is. Hence it is not a matter of necessity, in an important sense, that the bar is one metre in length.

5 I have argued this at some length in chapter 6 of my *Presupposition*.

6 See Hinton for a detailed discussion of this point in connection with perception and illusion.

Chapter 6

Creativity and Understanding

So far we have been concerned, roughly speaking, with the relatively narrow issue of grammatical knowledge and how it should be specified. Without by any means deserting this issue, we now shift to broader psychological issues — learning, association, dispositions, concept-possession, and others.

Any recent book about language will probably mention, and with an air of significance, that language is *creative* (or, to use another favoured expression, *productive*). This does not mean, as one might expect, that certain persons — poets, punsters, and orators, say — use language creatively. In the intended sense all fluent speakers are creative, and fully as creative as the Shelleys, the Johnsons, and the Ciceros among us. It is upon the fact of linguistic creativity that a case has been built against empiricist and behaviourist accounts of language and learning, and in favour of KLT and the new innateness hypothesis.

Actually, a whole number of claims are contained under the umbrella contention that language is creative; and I shall begin with two that, from our point of view, are less interesting. First, it is creative in the sense that there is no finite limit to the number of possible well-formed sentences. This is established by reflecting that there is no longest sentence.[1] Any number of clauses, for example, could be inserted into the frame 'John, who . . . . . . , died', beginning perhaps with 'John, who liked Mary, who ate the cake, which Peter gave his dog, to which . . . , died'. This is in no way a claim about human psychology. It is quite compatible with it that adults should only ever produce the small number of sentences they encountered before the age of ten. But the second claim is about humans, and it is, simply, that men do very often produce and understand sentences which neither they nor anyone else has previously produced.

Neither of these claims could have exciting consequences for psychology. The first might rule out certain theories of language which have no place for infinite embedding; and the second might outlaw the very crudest of stimulus-response accounts of learning. But the mere fact that people understand new sentences and that the sentences of a language are infinite in number could no more support KLT than the facts that people take steps and that there is no upper limit to the number of possible footsteps could support a similar thesis about unconscious knowledge of the rules of walking. But the more interesting 'creativity claims' are still to come.

The third claim is this: not only do people understand many sentences that are new to them, but a high proportion of these will be totally *unlike* any the people have previously encountered. At a point in his life, a speaker has learned the meaning of various sentences he has encountered, and these, we might say, form his 'learned corpus'. After that point he will produce and understand, immediately and accurately, many new sentences which are quite unlike any in the learned corpus. The implication drawn is that it is impossible, therefore, to explain how the new sentences are understood in terms of inductive generalization from, or empirical analogy with, the contents of the learned corpus.

> The sentences used in everyday discourse are not 'familiar sentences' or 'generalizations of familiar sentences' in terms of any known process of generalization. In fact, even to speak of 'familiar sentences' is an absurdity (Chomsky 1967 : p. 4).

Elsewhere Chomsky insists that to describe the process by which a person understands most new sentences as one of analogy is 'simply to give a name to what remains a mystery' (1968 : p. 30).

The actual processes employed in understanding new

sentences are allegedly those postulated by KLT. We understand a new sentence through engaging our knowledge of an abstract grammar. Even for KLT there is a sense in which we understand on the basis of the learned corpus, for knowledge of an abstract grammar partly results from encountering sentences in this corpus. It is not that we have inferred the rules of grammar from these sentences; rather we have used them to test the various hypotheses we constructed concerning the nature of our language. As the corpus grows, more and more false hypotheses will be eliminated, and it is by utilizing the remaining ones that we understand new sentences. There is a sense, too, in which, even for KLT, new sentences are similar to ones already encountered. For all sentences of the language have features of the abstract grammar speakers have internalized. The essential point is that new sentences need not be 'observably' similar to any in the corpus. The similarities may be of a highly abstract and 'unobservable' kind.

This third claim plays a crucial role, naturally, in the new innateness hypothesis. For the moment, let me simply quote Chomsky on this point:

> . . . empiricist speculations . . . have not provided any way to account for or even to express the fundamental fact about the normal use of language, namely the speaker's ability to produce and understand instantly new sentences that are not similar to those previously heard in any physically defined sense . . . nor obtainable from them by any sort of 'generalization' known to psychology or philosophy. It seems plain that language acquisition is based upon the child's discovery of . . . a deep and abstract theory — a generative grammar of his language. . . . A consideration of the character of the grammar that is acquired . . . leave(s) little hope that much of the structure of the language can be learned by an organism initially uninformed as to its general character (1965 : pp. 57-8).

It will be with this third claim, and its implications for knowledge and learning of language, that this chapter will be concerned.

There is a fourth 'creativity claim' which Chomsky sometimes runs together with the previous one, but which is, though related, distinct. This is the claim that speakers have 'the ability to produce and interpret new sentences in independence from 'stimulus control' — i.e. external stimuli or independently identifiable internal states' (1967 : p. 4). This is meant as a rebuttal of the view, attributed to Quine and Skinner, that knowledge of a language is a 'complex of dispositions to respond', or 'an associative net constructed by conditioned response'. It is not readily clear why this claim should be run together with the third. That sentences are understood through inductive generalization, and that sentence production is not under stimulus control, seem to be pretty different objections to two different positions. A connection between the two claims, though, might be made in this way: if sentence production is under stimulus control, then some of the eliciting stimuli and the uttered responses must be new, since speakers produce new sentences. Now if a new stimulus is to produce a correspondingly new response, through conditioning, then they must at least be similar to ones in the past; otherwise the conditioning could have no influence on the current situation. Also, since stimuli and responses must be observable, similarities between stimuli or responses must be observable ones. So, anyone who holds that sentence production is under stimulus control must be holding that new sentences are responses observably similar to ones elicited in the past by stimuli that are observably similar to current ones. However, the view that new sentences must be observably similar to previously encountered ones is precisely what is rejected by the third claim. Hence the third and fourth claims are related in that the position rejected by the fourth (viz. that sentences are under stimulus control) entails the position rejected by the third (viz. that new sentences are always observably similar to ones in the learned corpus). We take up the fourth claim in the next chapter.

The usual ways of making out the third claim, and of drawing anti-empiricist conclusions from it, are undoubtedly question-begging, since they presuppose just that unconscious knowledge of abstract grammar that we have been at some pains to criticize. But the arguments are misguided even when they are stated in ways that are not question-begging. Before arguing, at the end of the chapter, that the whole 'empiricist' vs. 'rationalist' debate over creativity is largely misconceived, I want to look in some detail at a presentation of the third claim. I hope the following is not an unfair summary of pp. 249-60 of Katz's *The Philosophy of Language:*

> A person who has learned what some sentences mean has come to pair sequences of sound with meanings (or, in the jargon, phonetic with semantic interpretations). This will involve recognizing various semantic 'elements' in the sentences, which are paired with certain sounds. The speaker's 'task' or 'problem' is to devise, on the basis of such learning, a set of rules or principles which will enable him to pair sounds with meanings in the future. By an empiricist account, these principles would be inductive generalizations from observed features of the learned sentences. They will take the form, 'Since this phonetic feature has been associated in the past with this semantic element, then it, or one closely analogous to it, must be associated with the same, or a closely analogous, semantic element on the present occasion'.

> . . . if the associationist theory is to successfully explain the case of language learning, the physical speech sounds, or utterances, from which the child acquires his knowledge of the rules of the linguistic description must contain, or be analyzable into, observable and distinguishable elements such that for each constituent of the meaning of an utterance whose meaning has been acquired there is an observable and distinguishable component of its phonetic shape with which that semantic constituent can be associated (p. 250).

But no such associationist theory can be correct, for a person who understands a new sentence will typically have to know its underlying structure; since, as we know, surface structure is such a poor guide to meaning. For example, the command 'Help the man!' is understood with 'you' as its subject; but there is no reflection of this feature at the surface, or phonetic, level. It follows that one cannot understand new sentences on the basis of generalizations connecting observable features with semantic elements — for features representable only at the level of deep structure are, while essential for understanding sentences, unobservable. In a narrow sense, only phonetic features are observable. In a more liberal sense, those surface features 'correlated' with phonetic shapes are also observable. But deep features, which are not closely correlated with sounds, cannot be observable by any stretch of the term. So the most a speaker could gain by inductive generalization would be rules relating surface features to meanings which, as we know, would not suffice for understanding sentential meanings fully.

> . . . since the observable structure of sentences is often quite severely impoverished from the point of view of semantic interpretation and since principles of inductive generalization add nothing structural or substantive to these structures on which they operate, it follows that such principles cannot account for the full range of semantic, as well as syntactic, properties on which the interpretation of sentences, essential to communication with them, depends (p. 256).

Katz's way of putting things clearly begs many questions. It presupposes, for example, that speakers know underlying structures, and that they follow complex, abstract rules. So completely are these questions begged that even the mythical empiricist or associationist rival is portrayed as accepting these presuppositions. His 'problem' is pictured as that of explaining how the child internalizes the rules of linguistic description so that the 'semantic content contributed by unobservable grammatical features becomes part of the full meaning of sentences' he understands (p. 255). Naturally, the rival fails to solve his 'problem'. But why should he conceive the problem along these lines? One who wishes to explain understanding of new sentences in terms of induction or analogy is extremely unlikely to grant that this will depend upon knowledge of deep, unobservable features, and the internalization of highly abstract rules.

But there are a number of peculiarities and difficulties I find in Katz's account, even if it is stated in less question-begging terms. These surround, first, the peculiar distinction between the observable and the unobservable which he draws, and second, the notions of meaning and understanding he employs.

a). *'observable' and 'unobservable'*: One could, I suppose, stipulate that, in the relevant area, 'observable' and 'unobservable' are to mean 'surface features' and 'deep features' respectively. Assuming a transformational grammar, it will then follow that sentences have both observable and unobservable features. But it is unclear how this stipulation should worry the empiricist. In the first place, the existence of unobservables is only troublesome for an empiricist psychology if it is taken that men are actually acquainted with them, have some knowledge of them. But, as I just pointed out, the empiricist is not likely to concede that the unobservables in question are objects of acquaintance or knowledge. He is more like to accept my arguments of the last chapter on this matter. Second, he could justifiably query whether deep features are unobservable in any useful or ordinary sense of that term; any sense that could have bearings on the traditional empiricist problem over unobservability. We were told, for example, that 'Help the man!' has an unobservable subject, represented only in underlying structure. Put in terms that do not beg questions, the point seems to be, simply, that the sentence contains no particular sound indicating to whom the command is addressed. Hence it is concluded, this latter 'feature' is unobservable. But this can be so only in the oddest sense of 'unobservable'. One might as well argue that it is an unobservable 'feature' of a letter that it is written to John if it does not begin with the greeting 'Dear John'. Someone can say this if he likes, but it will no longer follow that unobservable features are ones which cannot be ascertained through straightforward empirical, observational procedures. Clearly, there could be all sorts of observational clues showing us the letter was intended for John, and it is not obvious how the sentence without the spoken subject should create any more of a problem for the empiricist than the letter without the preliminary greeting.

(Parenthetically, I am unimpressed by that style of argument for transformational grammars which, relying on examples like 'Help the man!', demands a level of underlying structure that will contain the subjects (objects, etc.) recognized by speakers but not apparent in the spoken utterance. One might, non-facetiously, raise the following questions:

1. People can command by pointing a finger. So is the subject, 'you', deleted from the actual physical act, but present in the underlying structure of the pointing?

2. It has been argued by Ross that, for certain purposes, 'I' should be treated as the underlying subject of all sentences, which can be represented as having the form 'I V that. . . ' , where V is some illocutionary verb ('state', 'declare', 'ask', etc.). Are we to conclude that a speaker's stating, declaring, or questioning are unobservable features of utterances which the empiricist, with his crude reliance upon the senses, cannot account for?).

The following might be put forward to defend the way Katz has drawn the 'observable'/'unobservable' distinction. Suppose we start with a set of features that are paradigmatically observable, including the traditional 'secondary' qualities, as well as some of the 'primary' ones, like shape. Other features may be graded according to how closely their presence 'correlates' with the presence of paradigmatically observable ones. Those correlating highly will be relatively observable. In other words, if one can predict accurately that something having feature X will have the paradigmatically observable features A, B, . . .C, and vice-versa, then X is relatively observable. For example, the feature 'hirsute' will be relatively observable, since a man's being hairy correlates with certain paradigmatic features of colour, touch, shape, and so on. On the other hand, since there is little observably in common between pound notes and dimes, the feature of being a medium of financial exchange will be relatively unobservable.

Various remarks of Katz and Chomsky suggest they are employing the above consideration. Katz, taking phonetic

features as paradigmatically observable, says that other sentential features are observable only if they 'can be predicted
directly from . . . phonetic representation, and nothing else'
(p. 251). And Chomsky's reason for denying that an element
in deep structure is observable seems to be that 'it may have
no close point-by-point correlation to the phonetic realization'
(1968 : p. 27). This consideration, moreover, echoes a familiar
and traditional way of drawing the distinction between the
observable and the unobservable. For instance, Berkeley's
'mediately' perceivable items are those directly inferred from
the 'immediately' perceived items of sensory experience.

An example of this line of argument in action would
be the following: speakers understand the sentence 'John is
better at chess than Bill' to mean John's chess-playing is
better than Bill's chess-playing. But that this is the comparison
intended is unobservable, since there is no correlation between
the second term in the comparison and phonetic shape.
Phonetically, the sentence is just as similar to 'John is better at
chess than Bill is at skiing' as it is to 'John is better at chess
than Bill is at chess'.

I have three things to say about such arguments, and the
way of drawing the distinction between the observable and
the unobservable on which they rest. First, the whole talk of
speaker-hearers recognizing unobservable *features* of sentences
when they recognize the addressee of a command, or the
comparison intended, is perverse — not because they are
instead recognizing observable features, but because what is
being recognized are not features at all. At any rate, they are
not features in a sense which allows them to be contrasted
with, and categorized with, observable features such as the
pitch or duration of an utterance. To portray the speaker-
hearer's recognition as consisting in an inference from observable to unobservable features is, therefore, perverse. It is no
less peculiar than describing a man who sees a pile of bricks to
be suitable for building his wall as having inferred from the
observable features of the bricks to the 'unobservable feature'
of their suitability for wall-building. I do not see why the
empiricist should regard a person's recognizing to whom
a command is addressed, or the comparison intended between

John and Bill, as any more of a problem than the man's seeing the suitability of the bricks. If, on the perverse grounds that suitability, intended comparison, or direction of a command are not observable features, one insists that they are therefore unobservable features, then let us stress (i) they are not unobservable features of a sort which have traditionally caused problems for empiricists (like ethical properties, or properties of material substance), and (ii) recognition of such features in no way defies straightforward empirical explanation. Presumably our man's seeing the bricks are suitable for his wall will not resist explanation in terms of his past and present experiences.

Once this misleading talk about 'features' is dropped, the distinction is seen to be one between information about colours, shapes, sounds, etc. (together with information 'directly' predictable from this), and other information about the world. Put this way — and this is my second point — the distinction rests on an arbitrary decree as to what information is to count as observationally acquired. No doubt the idea that only information about colours, sounds, etc. is so acquired has a long history, but that does not make it the less suspect. If the title 'observational' is restricted in its scope in that way, then any number of unreal problems are generated. There is no general correlation, for instance, between a thing's having a certain colour, shape, texture, and so on, and its being a table. In appearance Pembrokes are not much like the latest contraptions in the foyer of a modern art gallery. But should we want to say that one cannot, through observation and past experience, tell that what is before one is a table? Again, since a human action can, typically, be performed through a wide variety of bodily movements, does it follow that actions are unobservables inferred from the 'hard' observational data gauged with our eyes and ears? No more, I think, need the empiricist accept that recognition of the addressee of a command, or of a comparison intended, cannot be achieved through observation and experience on the sole ground that what is recognized has no general or direct association with phonetic features. I shall suggest, shortly, some of the empirically respectable resources available for such recognition. The present point is, simply, that only an unwarranted and arbitrary restriction of the term 'observational' to refer to features of sound could justify treating such cases of recognition as cases beyond the powers of observation and experience to explain.

Third, and finally, the claim that speakers must be equipped with complex innate structures and principles, so as to explain their knowledge of features not directly correlated with phonetic ones, would seem, to say the least, premature. I can do no better than quote a passage of Goodman's that bears on this issue:

> One might argue that the shapes and colours in paintings are in some sense surface (obvious) features, while the features that identify a picture as by a certain artist or of a certain school or period are in some sense deep (or obscure). Yet we learn with rather few examples to make some of the latter rather subtle distinctions. Must the mind therefore have been endowed at birth with a 'schematism' of artistic styles? (1969 : p. 139).

The point, once more, is that only if we restrict the notion of 'observable' to surface features directly connected with sounds (or colours, in Goodman's analogy), are we tempted to invoke innate structures or schematisms to explain how the mind progresses beyond these features to others. The invocation in the case of understanding sentences is not, at face value, more plausible than the invocation of innately known artistic styles.

b). *'meaning'* and *'understanding'*: My second difficulty with Katz's presentation concerns his notions of meaning and understanding meanings. For Fodor and Katz, the meanings of sentences are given by semantic representations involving the provision of semantic readings, in terms of semantic 'markers' and projection rules, for sentential deep structures. But there is confusion here. A semantic reading, like a phrase marker, is simply a formula or set of symbols. As a formula, even if synonymous with the sentence of which it is a reading, it does not provide an account of or interpretation of the sentence's meaning. Katzian representations, like those in the notation of the predicate calculus, may be more perspicuous than the original sentences, and hence provide better bases for semantic interpretation — but they do not themselves provide them. Someone may be just as unable to interpret the representation as the sentence for which it is a representation.

What is missing from Katz's account is any mention of communicative intentions and of truth conditions, which must figure in providing accounts of sentential meanings. My concern in making these unsatisfactorily brief remarks is not purely semantic. Rather, I want to show that by ignoring the role that intentions and truth conditions play in accounting for meanings, Katz is overlooking factors which play an essential part in learning language and in aiding understanding of new sentences. The best way to show this is in connection with various examples of understanding new sentences that Katz and Chomsky discuss.

(i)   *'Help the man!'*: For Katz this cannot be understood, as addressed to *you,* because of any observable similarity between it and 'You help the man!', since it is equally similar to 'No one help the man!' or 'Everyone help the man!'. Hence it must be based on grasping some unobservable relation between them.

Now it can be granted that if hearers had nothing to go on but phonetic similarity to sentences encountered in the past, they would have a problem in understanding such a sentence for the first time. A future historian of the dead English language would, equally, have trouble in understanding 'Help the man!' at first, since its orthographic shape would not tell him of what it is a contraction. But when we remind ourselves that understanding a sentence has something to do with grasping the speaker's intentions, than a whole range of other clues and evidence come into play. First, there is the context of the utterance. If I'm the only person in the room, or if the speaker is staring right at me, how else am I to understand his command except as addressed to me? Second, there is the manner of the utterance — the tone in which it is made, or the facial expressions accompanying it. If 'Help the man!' is said in an anxious, sympathetic way, I am not likely to interpret it as meaning that no one should help the man. Obviously, there are many other ways in which a hearer may be helped in understanding what a speaker intends.

(ii) *'John is better at chess than Bill'*: The empiricist, allegedly, has a problem in explaining how this sentence is immediately understood as comparing John's chess to Bill's chess, and not to his skiing, scrabble, or seducing (see p. 109). But, once more, let us remind ourselves that understanding the speaker's meaning is a matter of grasping his intentions (or certain of them). In gauging speakers' intentions, we are necessarily tolerant in that we assume, generally, that their words are suitable vehicles for carrying out those intentions. Naturally we have to revise this assumption in the case of some speakers on various occasions, but unless we generally made it we could not have any reason to interpret what a man is saying in one way rather than another. Such a presumption plays a large role in how we understand sentences. The utterer of the sentence in question *might*, for all the hearer encountering that sort of sentence for the first time can tell for sure, be comparing John's chess with Bill's skiing or seducing. But if he is, there was nothing about his utterance which could possibly convey that intention. Since the only activity mentioned was chess, it cannot be reasonable for the hearer, given his tolerant presumption vis-a-vis speakers, to interpret the sentence as doing anything but comparing one man's chess with another man's chess. We have the same sort of reason for interpreting the sentence in that way as we have for treating 'Yes' as a reply to an immediately preceding question. The person *might* be answering a question asked him three years earlier; but unless we have given up, in his case, the presumption that what is said is a reasonable guide to the speaker's intentions in communication, that interpretation will not be a genuine option.

(iii) *'John is $\begin{Bmatrix} eager \\ easy \end{Bmatrix}$ to please'*: When Chomsky and Katz talk of understanding a sentence, they often mean recognition of the paraphrases it permits or of the operations that can be performed on its constituents. 'John is easy to please' is understood differently from 'John is eager to please' in the sense that paraphrases of the forms 'It is . . . to please John'

113

or 'Pleasing John is . . . ' are permissible only where the blank is replaced by 'easy'. Also an operation resulting in 'John's eagerness to please . . . ', but not 'John's easiness to please . . . ', is acceptable. How, it is asked, can the empiricist explain such recognition and acceptance on first encounters with these sentences? For phonetically, and in 'observable' respects, 'John is easy to please' is just as similar to the previously encountered sentences 'John is willing (unwilling, keen, etc.) to please' as to the previously encountered 'John is hard (difficult, unpleasant, etc.) to please' — yet it is understood along the lines of the latter alone.

I am puzzled by the view that the empiricist has a serious problem on his hands here. First, granted that 'John is easy to please' is similar, in obvious ways, to 'John is willing (unwilling, keen, eager, etc.) to please', why is it assumed that this would encourage a tendency, in lieu of recognizing deep structural differences, to understand (i.e. paraphrase) them similarly? For, after all, there is also an obvious difference between the sentences. One contains 'easy' and the other(s) contains 'willing' ('unwilling' etc.). There is no great reason to think that the similarity in sentential frames should outweigh the difference between the adjectives so as to encourage a tendency, were experience the only guide, to paraphrase them similarly. If I had a butler he might bring me my eggs and my mail on similar silver platters, but I am not tempted to treat the eggs and the mail similarly just because they appear in similar 'frames'. Equally, 'cattle' and 'rattle' have obvious similarities, but I am not tempted, in lieu of deep structural knowledge, to say 'cattling' as well as 'rattling', 'it cattled' as well as 'it rattled'. Second, it is myopic to suppose that nothing in the speaker's experience could guide him in paraphrasing the two sentences differently. If he had never encountered the relevant adjectives except in frames like 'John is . . . to please', then he might have a problem in knowing whether to interpret 'easy', say, along the lines of 'willing' and 'unwilling' or along the lines of 'hard' and 'unpleasant'. But, of course, he has encountered all such words in innumerable other contexts as well. He knows what the words mean. He knows that 'John is willing' or 'John is happy' are meaningful in a way that

'John is hard' or 'John is easy' are not (unless 'hard' and 'easy' are taken to mean 'severe' and 'easy-going', or something like that). He has come to interpret sentences beginning with 'It is easy . . . ' or 'It is hard . . . ' in way that he has not come to interpret sentences beginning 'It is willing . . . ' or 'It is eager . . . ' (unless 'it' is a pronoun referring to an animal or an hermaphrodite). In other words, he can rely upon a rich history of interpretation to help him interpret, to paraphrase, newly encountered sentences like 'John is easy to please'. If all I knew about the objects on my butler's platters was that they appeared on his platters, I might not know what to do with them — rather as the unsophisticated dinner guest might not know what to do with an artichoke on the plate before him. But if I have learned what the one object, a slice of toast is, and what the other object, a letter, is, I shall not be tempted to treat them alike — to eat the letter, or open the toast to find a message inside.

The general point over the last few pages has been that KLT only derives support, *via* the discrediting of empiricism, from linguistic creativity, if arbitrary limitations are imposed on the range of observations and experience that people can call upon to aid them in understanding new sentences.[2]

The terms 'similarity' and 'analogy' have cropped up a good deal over the preceding pages, as indeed they do in the relevant literature. I have made no attempt to elucidate them — and nor, unfortunately, have Chomsky and other proponents of KLT. But one is bound to worry about his use of the terms when he says, for example, that it is extremely unlikely that the reader will have previously encountered a sentence analogous to 'I disapprove of John's drinking'. I should think that a quick perusal of *Winnie-The-Pooh* would show that young children are likely to have encountered any number of sentences 'analogous' to that one in some not obviously perverse sense. Chomsky's lack of interest in elucidating these terms is surprising given the vital roles they play in his refutation of empiricist accounts of creativity. For the refutation, remember, revolves around the claim that there is insufficient observable similarity between many new sentences and ones in the learned corpus for our understanding of the former to

115

be explained on the basis of the latter.

I am going to argue that misconceptions over these notions vitiate the whole attack on empiricism and the move towards KLT. I shall grant that the empiricist position as portrayed by its critics is untenable, but the natural conclusion should be that a different portrait is needed, together with a reappraisal of the nature of the whole debate.

In chapter 4, I dismissed what I dubbed the 'baby scientist' view of the language learner — according to which the learner, like the scientist, devises and tests, on the basis of various observable data, principles and hypotheses which he projects in order to deal with new instances. For one thing, as Hamlyn notes, once we describe the encountered utterances as 'data' for the child, we are already presupposing considerable theoretical sophistication on his part; since something serves as a datum for a person only to the extent that he sees it as relative to some theory (e.g. as confirming it, or falsifying it). The point I want to stress now is that this view is perverse *whatever* the nature of the hypotheses and principles is taken to be — whether as 'inductivist', 'associationist', or 'abstractionist' ones acceptable to empiricists, or as ones concerning deep, unobservable features postulated by KLT. If it is absurd to suppose a young child is unconsciously formulating hypotheses about unobservable sub-atomic structures from the 'data' of his baby-food, it is scarcely less absurd to suppose he is unconsciously devising 'inductivist' hypotheses which he projects on encountering his next dish of milk-pudding. To represent the child's position in this way would, as Hamlyn remarks, be like foisting the 'other minds' problem upon him when he identifies human actions. The 'data' would be observable bodily movements, on the basis of which the child would be constructing hypotheses relating movements to actions, which he then projects in identifying new actions. Now this picture would be unacceptable whether the hypotheses are meant to be of an 'assocationist' type, or of a different type concerning unobservable occurrences underlying actions. Philosophers can burden themselves with the problem of 'other minds', but they should not burden the child with it.

Given the care and love that a mother devotes to her

child (or if not this at least some attitude which is appropriate to a person) how could there even be a problem for the child about the difference between people and things? (p. 192-3).

The above consideration is crucial; for the empiricist position, as portrayed by Chomsky and Katz, is precisely that the child understands new sentences by projecting inductive hypotheses, formed through abstractionist operations on the data of his learned corpus. Now this position is, I am sure, untenable — for reasons that Chomsky and Katz give in addition to the kind just sketched. But the implication is not that we should embrace KLT, for that shares the major defect of the position under attack. Nor does it follow that empiricism is untenable, since the position may be a caricature of what an empiricst should be holding. Certainly I should consider my own position, as it emerges in this and the following chapter, as warranting the title 'empiricist' — though, perhaps those with a more purified idea of empiricism might protest.

Suppose the empiricist were to embrace the 'baby scientist' view, attributed to him by Chomsky and Katz. Then he might argue as follows: the child has heard his mother and father utter the sentences 'My leg hurts' and 'My arm hurts', and he has learned them to the extent of recognizing the situation his parents intended to describe by these utterances. One day the child bangs his nose and says, with apparent understanding, 'My nose hurts'. Our 'empiricist' will suggest that the child's intelligent utterance results from something like the following hypothesis that he has erected on the basis of his parents' utterance: Whenever a part of a person's anatomy hurts him, it is correct for him to utter a sentence whose first word is 'my', whose second word is the name of the part involved, and whose last word is 'hurts'. A resulting sentence will be analogous to the ones produced by the parents, since it is identical to theirs except for the anatomical name which, since it is an anatomical name, is obviously analogous to those they employed.

It seems to me that any puzzle our 'empiricist' felt over how the child understood the new sentence, 'My nose hurts', remains — in a new guise — after the proferred explanation in

117

terms of the suggested hypothesis. For there are an indefinite number of hypotheses that might have been constructed and projected on the basis of the 'data' available to the child in the form of his parents' utterances. Some of these would, and some would not, warrant the child in thinking that 'My nose hurts' is an appropriate vehicle for describing his own predicament. He might, for example, have inducted the following hypothesis: Whenever *my parents* hurt in some part of their anatomy, it is correct for *them* to say 'My . . . hurts'. Or the following: Whenever a person hurts in *one of a pair* of anatomical parts, it is correct for him to say 'My . . . hurts'. Neither hypothesis would allow him to say 'My nose hurts' as a description of his injury – though the second would allow him to say 'My eye hurts' or 'My arm hurts' when it is his eye or arm that is hurt. Clearly, the 'data' which the child has to go on severely *underdetermine* the choice between various hypotheses compatible with the data, and hence do not determine what further sentences are 'similar' or 'analogous' to the ones providing the data. For whether a new sentence is similar or analogous to previous ones is supposed to depend on its being covered by a projected hypothesis which has abstracted relevant features from these previous ones. So, any mystery there might have been over the child's understanding a new sentence as a result of having learned others will survive as a mystery over his having managed to hit upon just that hypothesis which enables him to understand it properly. So interpolating the hypothesis construction has got us nowhere. Perhaps this point is implicit in some of Chomsky's criticisms of 'inductivist' accounts of learning and understanding. But before we jump to the hasty conclusion that the child must be constructing hypotheses or principles of a quite different calibre, immune from the problem of underdetermination by observed 'data', let us note two things:

First, the problem of underdetermination is a quite general one, so there is no *special* problem raised for the empiricist by the underdetermination of linguistic hypotheses. I recognize this object before me as a cigarette, as relevantly like objects I have encountered in the past and learned to call cigarettes. If this is thought to require explanation in terms of my having abstracted from my encounters a hypothesis which I project in the present instance, it should also require explanation how I hit upon just the right hypothesis. I might have hypothesized that cigarettes are objects that must come in packets, or that they must have glowing ends. If, on the other hand, it is not thought a problem worth considering how I hit upon the right hypothesis, neither should it be regarded as a problem how I identified new cigarettes *without* the interpolation of such a hypothesis. Certainly the *least* plausible move would be to postulate hypotheses of a quite non-empirical type, concerning the 'unobservable' features of cigarettes, and to suppose I must have constructed these and be projecting them in new instances.

Second, it is often not so much unhelpful as absurd to suppose that a person's recognizing new instances results from his having formed general hypotheses about shared features on the basis of 'data'. And this is so whether the features involved are obvious or 'deep', observable or unobservable, and whether the hypotheses are 'associationist' or highly abstract. This will be the case wherever the similarity between instances does not consist in the the sharing of features by them. The point can be illustrated by reference to an important area of linguistic behaviour — which, incidentally is 'creative' in a more normal sense than so far encountered. I refer to the ability to use, and recognize the appropriateness of, words occurring in various metaphorical ways.[3] For example, it is not only physical objects, according to their thermal properties, which are warm, cold, freezing, etc.. Facial expressions, tones of voice, personalities, and paintings can all be warm or cold. It is implausible to treat such uses as merely homophonic, for not only are they found in many languages, but there is remarkable agreement among people on how to extend metaphors in contexts that are new to them.[4] But what is it that makes a voice or facial expression similar or analogous to a refrigerator or a greenhouse? What seems certain is that a person's finding a relevant similarity does not result from his having abstracted those features in common to all things literally described by 'warm' or 'cold', and his finding that

119

some of these belong to the things he then goes on to call warm or cold in metaphorical senses. True, a cold voice, like a block of ice, can chill you or send shivers up you — but it is a metaphorical chill, and they are metaphorical icicles. It seems to me there is just no answer to the question 'by virtue of what features of voices, facial expressions, refrigerators, and blocks of ice are all of them counted as cold?'. This conclusion should create less alarm than it might at first once we reflect that it is a conclusion we are anyway forced to when discussing how words, in their quite literal senses, become applied to new instances. As Goodman has argued — most recently in his *Languages of Art* — recognizing a new surface as (thermally) cold is not something we do by virtue of having abstracted features shared by previously encountered cold surfaces, and finding this new one also shares them. No doubt an explanation of some sort can be given, as to why people classify things in the ways they do — explanations in terms of shared physical properties of things, or the common physiological effects they have upon us. But these are not characteristics by virtue of which *we* rate new instances to be similar to others. They are not *our* reasons for classifying in one way rather than another. To repeat, it is the general idea that new instances can only be identified by virtue of features they share with previously encountered ones which is misplaced — and it does not matter whether the features in question are those admissible for an empiricist, or the abstract, 'deep' ones appealed to by a KLT opponent.

So, the 'empiricist's' position, as portrayed by Chomsky and Katz, is indeed untenable. But it follows neither that empiricism must be rejected, nor that we should immediately embrace the alternative offered us by KLT. I want to emphasise this in connection with some of Chomsky's remarks, which can now be seen as compounds of truth and error.

a). He remarked, as we noted earlier, that to call the processes by which speakers understand new sentences one of analogy is 'to give a name to what remains a mystery'. If this means that empiricist psycholinguists have not succeeded in specifying hypotheses that speakers could plausibly be reckoned to have constructed, through abstraction from 'data', and projected onto new instances, what he says in true — but extremely misleading. To say that the psycholinguists have not succeeded implies they have failed where others might succeed. But there is nothing to succeed in. For speakers do not — generally at least — understand new sentences on the basis of any hypotheses which they have constructed for themselves, whether 'inductivist' ones or those of an abstract generative grammar. Misleading, therefore, is the reference to the 'processes' involved in understanding new sentences. If these are supposed to be ones of constructing, testing, and applying hypotheses and principles, then there just are not any processes involved at all. And misleading, finally, is the reference to a 'mystery'. This implies there is an answer to the question 'What is the nature of the principles on the basis of which, speakers understand new sentences?', which empiricists have failed to answer. But there is not an answer. Speakers just do identify new sentences as similar to others — and appeal to principles they have internalized is sometimes absurd, and nearly always unhelpful. If there is a mystery, it is, like the 'mystery of nature', one with which the empiricist can live.

b).   Chomsky, as we well know, repeatedly invokes innate factors to account for our understanding of new sentences. If this meant only that understanding is not to be explained in terms of 'inductivist' hypothesis construction, that there is *something* about human beings which makes them classify and identify in the ways they do, then it is unobjectionable. But if it means, as it does for Chomsky, that we must ascribe to speakers an innate grasp of various principles enabling them to relate new instances to old, then it shares the major defect with the doctrine it replaces. Obviously there is *something* about men — something not learned, something innate if you like — which enables them to classify and identify. But there is no reason for thinking this to be constituted by the principles and structures of universal grammar.

c).   In various places, he has held the empiricist's notions of 'similarity' and 'analogy' to be vacuous. Interpreted in a certain way, his charge contains an important element of truth — a truth, I think, that Wittgenstein strove to express in his remarks about 'sameness'. Unless we know how people

121

actually do classify new cases, what they do find it appropriate and natural to do in new instances, to claim that things are similar or analogous lacks substance. Even where we are able to formulate a rule, and so judge that things are similar if they fall under it, our formulation and judgment have empirical content only to the extent that we know how the rule is actually interpreted and applied. In every case, as Wittgenstein says, a rule can be variously interpreted. Now if Chomsky were saying that — in the absence of telling how people actually do interpret new sentences, paraphrase them, or find it appropriate to use them — claims about their similarity or analogy to others would be vacuous, then he would be right. But, put like this, it becomes clear that we lend substance to the notions of 'similarity' and 'analogy' not by inventing similarities and rules of a non-empirical variety, but by making people's actual behaviour — their interpretations, their paraphrases, their natural responses, etc. — the very criterion for similarity and analogy. And this the empiricist can do. It will not be vacuous to claim that 'My nose hurts' is analogous to 'My arm hurts' or 'My leg hurts' for the simple reason that speakers do treat it analogously — by paraphrasing it similarly, responding to it in similar ways, and so on. Put crudely, the point is this: the speaker does not deal with the new case appropriately by recognizing similarities between it and previous ones. Rather it is his, and other speakers', dealing with it in some ways and not others, that makes it similar, in the relevant respect, to the previous ones.

There might seem an unpalatable element of subjectivism, or even idealism, in the above remarks. Are we not making similarities and analogies functions of what people think they are? Well, no subjectivism is involved in the sense of implying that each individual is a sovereign authority on the similarities and analogies that surround him. For his judgments and behaviour may be compared with, and assessed by reference to, the judgments and behaviour of men at large — or, at any rate, of men in his linguistic community. But if the terms 'subjectivist' and 'idealist' serve merely to highlight that, in the last resort, it is mass agreement in judgment, classification, and behaviour which determine the similarities and analogies there are, then I do not find the subjectivism and idealism involved unpalatable.

Notes to Chapter 6

1   Since writing this book I have read an article by Ziff (1974) in which he argues persuasively against the view that a sentence in a natural language can be well formed once it passes a certain length.

2   Once it is appreciated how much the speaker-hearer has to go on, besides having experienced 'similar' sentences in the past, in interpreting new sentences, then various facts often cited in favour of KLT and the new innateness hypothesis, can be seen in a quite different light. For example, Lenneberg sees support for innate predetermination in the fact that children of dumb parents are only slightly retarded in their speech development. But, as Campbell and Wales have argued, this may only show that proponents of KLT have overvalued the role that a certain kind of linguistic experience should play on empiricist premises. They go on to point out that past successes in carrying out communicative intentions may play a role quite equal to bombardment by parental utterances.

3   Metaphorical usage is important precisely because it is so much more widespread than often imagined. Lest anyone think it rare and casual, let him feast his eyes on the following passage, not at all atypical of music criticism, and reflect how difficult it would be to avoid all the metaphors. (I have italicized the obviously metaphorical occurrences).:

> The viola is not a *forthcoming soloist*. Its tone is *slender* and easily *covered,* and it *speaks* best in a pitch area *densely populated* by more *vociferous* instruments. There is a strong *rhetorical vein* in the piece; in the viola's long, *striding* theme . . . in its brisk *exclamatory sallies*. A *tough,* almost *obtuse* kind of *personality* seems to *speak* through this music and the *voice* gains *force* and *vitality* at each *utterance* (Stanley Sadie : *The Times*).

4   Roger Brown, for instance, asked a number of musical philistines to rate some opera singers' voices according to their 'warmth' or 'coldness'. There was remarkable agreement in the ratings.

Chapter 7

Dispositions and Knowledge

In this chapter I move from attack to counter-attack. For I want to sketch a certain view of linguistic knowledge and to defend it against various objections levelled by proponents of KLT. In fact, the connection between this view and KLT is not obvious. Certainly, though, proponents of KLT have taken it to be one of diametrical opposition, and I too think there is an important connection. But even if we are all wrong about this, the topic is of sufficient interest to examine, independently of any putative connection with KLT.

The view I want to sketch and defend — I do not think it warrants the title 'theory' — is neither new nor, I fear, particularly exciting. Its one merit, I hope, is that it is substantially correct. It is a view which, in its most general form at least, is found fairly obviously in Ryle and less obviously in Wittgenstein (or so I suspect). More recently, it has been explicitly stated by Quine, and less explicitly by several other philosophers.[1] It is a view, too, which still dominates the thinking of some psycholinguists — notably Skinner — despite the prevalence in most recent psycholinguistic writings of KLT.

I will call the view in question the 'disposition account' (DA). Language, writes Quine, can be regarded as

> the complex of present dispositions to verbal behaviour, in which speakers of the same language have perforce come to resemble one another (1960 : p. 27).

Linguistic competence, says Harman, is 'knowledge in the sense of knowing how to do something; it is ability' (1967 : p. 81). A person who knows a language is one with a certain complex of dispositions towards verbal behaviour, a person with the ability or 'know how' to perform in certain ways under certain conditions. Naturally, these dispositions will be enormously varied — ranging from the disposition to employ and respond to a word in particular ways, which constitutes knowing what it means, to the disposition to detect irregularities in sentence forms, which partly constitutes knowledge of some portion of syntax.

To portray knowledge of a language in this way in no sense involves denying that speakers typically have other knowledge, knowledge *that,* as well. But in the first place, statements of the form 'A knows that . . . ' are often best elucidated in terms of ability or know how. If a person is unable to say what a word means, or is not ready to accept any particular definition, yet nevertheless displays a grasp of its meaning in his impeccable, everyday use of it, then to say of him 'He knows that the word means . . . ' can only be to say he has a certain ability and know how. Second, uncontroversial items of irreducible knowledge *that* — where, in other words, the person can actually avow what he is said to know — are, typically, luxuries earned by reflection on one's speech or through instruction, and are not required for a person to be said to know the language. I may know how passives are derived from actives in English; I can state the rule. But even if I could not, I would not, on these grounds alone, be disqualified as someone who does not know English; since I can still form passives. There are some propositions, naturally, which we would expect any fluent speaker to recognize as true — those, for example, which state the meanings of well-known and easily definable words, or ones like 'Most English plurals end in 's''. But if a speaker did not, I do not think we would conclude he does not know English. Our puzzel over such a person would be a general one about his intelligence and powers of reflection and observation. How could a person be so stupid or so unobservant not to agree that most of the plurals he utters end in 's'?

It is with the general dispositional account just sketched,

and not any particular version of it, that I will be concerned. For example, I shall not take stands on issues like the following:

a) *Precisely* what behaviour must a person, in order to know his language, be disposed towards? I will not discuss whether, say, being able to provide (even very rough) paraphrases is necessary to knowing their meanings.

b) *Precisely* what conditions must elicit verbal behaviour for it to be said the person had a disposition to that behaviour, and hence some linguistic knowledge.

In connection with the second question, it is clear there are limits on the allowable conditions. The fact that the conditions involved in my spending two years at a Biarritz language academy would result in my producing sentences in Portugese or Dutch would hardly show that, at the beginning of the period, I knew Portugese and Dutch. On the other hand, we would not treat a person's failure to respond with understanding to an eliciting eighty-four word question as evidence for his not knowing the language.

Certainly DA, even in the general form I have taken it, requires more elaboration for our purposes, but the best place for this is when we come to look at various objections to it. Before that, however, I want to look at the relation between DA and KLT, and especially at the relation between DA and the fourth of the 'creativity claims' (see p. 102 ff).

Chomsky and others take DA to be incompatible with KLT, and to be, in fact, the rival account they are most anxious to discredit.

> . . . it is important to realize that in no technical sense of these words can language use be regarded as a matter of 'habit' or can language be regarded as a 'complex of dispositions to respond' (1967 : p. 4).

Elsewhere Chomsky rejects as 'unwarranted' the assumption that 'language is a "habit structure" or a network of associative connections, or that knowledge of language is merely a matter of "knowing how", a skill expressible as a system of dispositions to respond' (1968 : p. 22). And in both places he goes on to recommend KLT as the proper alternative.

Ignoring his reference to the 'technical' senses of the relevant terms (whatever they are meant to be), and for the moment, his mention of habits alongside dispositions, the question arises as to why Chomsky is so anxious to reject DA — or, at any rate, to reject it as an apparently necessary prelude to instating KLT. For it is not obvious, at first sight, why it should not be claimed that a person who knows his language has a set of dispositions to behave *and* has 'internalized' an abstract grammar. It might seem, indeed, that the two accounts are at rather different levels; that, perhaps, while DA reveals what is meant by knowing a language, KLT provides an explanation of that knowledge by accounting for the genesis of the dispositions. This possibility was canvassed in chapter 2.

Let me use an analogy to throw a light on what, I think, is the relation between DA and KLT. A man sees a yellow patch. One philosopher describes this as being disposed to discriminate and classify in certain ways, while a second describes it as the occurrence of some private, 'phenomenal' item. So far there is no incompatibility; perhaps the disposition is caused by the occurrence. Suppose, though, the first philosopher insists there is nothing more to be said about seeing something besides specification of the perceiver's dispositional state; that reference to private data serves neither to analyse what seeing is, nor to explain a person's discriminatory abilities.₂ Now the second philosopher need not, in strict logic, deny that the perceiver is in a dispositional state. All he has to show is that reference to this state cannot be a complete account of what seeing is. Still, by far his most effective strategy will be to demonstrate that reference to dispositions is just out of place — for then his own suggestion could be seen, not as a supplement to an account of seeing, but as a necessary replacement for a mistaken account. Similarly, it is when the proponent of DA insists there is nothing that need be said about knowing a language other than a description of dispositions that his opponent must beg to differ. Once more, all the proponent of KLT *needs* to do is show that DA is incomplete. But his most effective strategy will be to demonstrate that DA is mistaken, that knowing a language has nothing to do with behavioural dispositions. For then KLT would seem an inevitable alternative to DA, not a supplement to it. It is only if Chomsky sees the relation between DA and KLT along these lines — assuming he has not misconstrued DA — that I can understand his anxiety to discredit DA as a prelude to embracing KLT.

The question also arises as to why Chomsky thinks he is refuting DA by establishing the fourth of the 'creativity claims' — the claim that sentence production and interpretation is not under 'stimulus-control'. After all, he often insists he is concerned only with competence, not performance; but the issue of stimulus-control seems to be about performance. I have already tried to suggest why he feels the need to reject the idea of stimulus-control (p. 104). It contradicts his account of language learning. If my sentence is a response elicited by some stimulus then, so it is argued, it must be 'observably' similar to responses previously elicited by like stimuli. Since in Chomsky's view many of the sentences I produce are not 'observably' similar to ones I have produced in the past, the stimulus- control account must be wrong. This issue, I hope, was dealt with in the last chapter. That he takes the challenge to the idea of stimulus-control to be a challenge to DA stems, I can only think, from an historical connection between dispositional theories and S-R theories — a connection that still persists in the writings of, say, Skinner. For Skinner, linguistic competence would consist in dispositions to responses caused by current stimuli as a result of a process of operant conditioning. Now it is true that talk of dispositions would be idle in the absence of some account of the sort of conditions under which the relevant behaviour, confirming the presence of the dispositions, is likely to be exhibited. But there is no necessity to regard these conditions along traditional S-R lines. There is no necessity, for example, why the dispositionalist should not include among the conditions what would be regarded as speaker's reasons, rather than mechanistic causes, for saying one thing rather than another. Nor, as we shall see, need he adopt Skinner's particular view about how conditions come, through conditioning, to elicit behaviour. (Parenthetically, I think we can see in Chomsky's concern with stimulus-control an admission — despite his pronouncements to the contrary — that performance factors are crucial to the notion of competence. Competence, I shall suggest, cannot possibly be gauged independently · of a speaker's performances under certain conditions).

I now turn to the various objections that have been levelled against DA:

1). Several writers[3] take as an objection to DA the failure of reinforcement (and related processes of traditional learning theory) to explain how a person comes to know a language. But the relevance of this consideration is lost upon me. Historically, those who have advocated something like DA might have gone on to explain the genesis of dispositions in terms of reinforcement, imitation, or the like. But there is no conceptual connection here, and *I* certainly do not intend DA to be committed to any particular doctrine about the genesis of dispositions. All that is excluded is the idea that they derive from prior theoretical knowledge of the kind postulated by KLT. Whether they originate through instruction, reinforcement, on the basis of a single experience, or as a result of unknown developments in the nervous system, is left open. The most reasonable guess, I should think, is that different dispositions arise in different ways. Some, like the tendency to employ a certain word in certain circumstances, may have resulted from a single experience of observing the pairing of a word and object, rather as one's tendency to avoid snakes may have resulted from a single and unpleasant encounter with an adder. Others, like employing appropriate conventional greetings, might require a good deal of social reinforcement to instil. It is reasonable to suppose, too, that reinforcement plays a larger role the younger the speakers are. Quine remarks that after a certain age the child's 'further learning of language becomes independent of operant behaviour even on the speaking side; and then, with little or no deliberate encouragement on the part of his elders, he proceeds to amass language hand over fist' (1960 : p. 82).

While I regard the reinforcement issue as irrelevant to the acceptability or otherwise of DA, and while I hold no particular brief for reinforcement theories, I do think it worth remarking that objections levelled against these theories by proponents of KLT are often question-begging or totally inconclusive. Fodor, for instance, writes:

> . . . the peculiarly abstract relation between base structures and sentences unfits any of the usual learning mechanisms for explaining their assimilation (1966 : p. 113).

And Slobin says:

> Could this schedule of reinforcement result in grammatical speech? Conceivably it could, but it would tell us nothing of the process whereby the child arrived at the underlying notions of grammar which would make correct performance possible (p. 57).

But whether speakers 'assimilate' base structures, or 'arrive at' underlying grammatical notions, is precisely what can be disputed. If speakers do this, reinforcement theories no doubt fail — but if the arguments of this book are accepted then speakers do not do this, and reinforcement theories remain so far untouched. Again, it is sometimes thought to be strong evidence against reinforcement that children 'overregularize' their speech.[4] If reinforcement explained speech one would expect, so it is argued, the child to say 'caught' and 'taught' and not 'catched' and 'teached', since only his utterances of the first two are positively reinforced. But it is typical, in fact, for children to utter the second two. This argument relies on a particular view about how reinforcement might be expected to work, and a reply could be that since the child has been reinforced on innumerable occasions for adding '-ed' to verbs, this will outweigh, and should be expected to outweigh, the occasions on which he is reinforced for correctly adding irregular affixes. Only if, implausibly, we credit the child with already having distinguished regular from irregular verbs would we expect reinforcement for irregular inflecting to counteract reinforcement for adding '-ed'.

2). There is another argument which appears originally against reinforcement theories and is then directed against DA. It is suggested in Chomsky's frequent practice of using 'habit' and 'disposition' as if they were interchangeable, or at least similar in what they imply (see p. 126). Presumably I can only be in the habit of uttering a certain sentence if I frequently utter that sentence. Hence if the sentences I produce after a certain age are ones uttered through habit then they must all be ones I have uttered before, in which case my repertoire of sentences would not only be finite but positively small. Chomsky thinks DA results in a similiarly false conclusion since he says of the claim that language is a complex of present dispositions that it is 'inconsistent with a truism . . . that language is an infinite set of sentences. . . . A network derived by the postulated mechanisms must be finite; it can, in fact, contain only the sentences to which a person has been exposed (repeatedly and under similar circumstances)' (1968-9 : p. 57).

The point about the 'postulated mechanisms' of reinforcement and conditioning appears to be this: if my producing a sentence is the result of such mechanisms then it must be one I have produced (repeatedly) in the past, otherwise I could not have been reinforced for producing *it*. This is a strange point. Any reinforcement theorist is surely going to insist that it is reinforcement of this behaviour *or* relevantly similar behaviour in the past which explains its present occurrence. Now the repertoire of behaviour relevantly similar to this behaviour can be indefinitely large. It will be replied, no doubt, that the notion of 'relevantly similar behaviour' is vacuous — but then we are back with the issue I tried to resolve in the last chapter.

Even if, moreover, Chomsky were right in supposing that reinforcement theories entailed the finiteness and paucity of a person's linguistic repertoire, it is impossible to see how this could affect DA, which is not wedded to any particular doctrine of reinforcement. If dispositions are thought of as akin to habits, of course, the dice are unfairly loaded. But not everything a person is disposed towards is something he does as a matter of habit. If all men of violent disposition were habitually violent, the world would be a sorrier place than it in fact is. While a person cannot do a large, let alone an infinite, number of things habitually, there is no similar limit to the number of dispositions he may have.

Even a humble lump of sugar can have an indefinitely large number of dispositions. That is, there is no limit to the number of true conditionals describing how it would behave under certain circumstances. No doubt there are habitual kinds of linguistic behaviour — conventional greetings, say, or uxorial grumbles — but it is not faintly suggested by DA that all or most linguistic dispositions are like these.

3). Chomsky asks

> . . . what point can there be to a definition of 'language' that makes language vary with mood, personality, brain lesions, eye injuries, gullibility, nutritional level, knowledge and belief, in the way in which 'dispositions to respond' will vary under these and numerous other relevant conditions? . . . .What a person does or is likely to do and what he knows may be related, in some way that cannot, for the moment, be made precise; the relation is, however, surely in part a factual and not a strictly conceptual one (1968-9 : p. 65).

Let me begin with the second part of the passage. The point seems to be that even if linguistic behaviour were evidence for a person's knowing a language it could not possibly explain what is meant by such knowledge. Well, I have never said that knowing something about one's language is always equivalent to a disposition, for I have granted that speakers typically possess a good deal of knowledge *that*, of an uncontroversial kind which they are ready, willing, and able to avow. I added, however, that knowledge like this is a luxury inessential for counting as one who knows his language. When we turn to knowing *how* (and the cases of knowing *that* which are best elucidated as knowing *how*), then I cannot see that linguistic behaviour is merely evidence for it. I do not want to get embroiled in the question of whether 'He knows English' means the same as a description of a person's dispositions. The problem here is not so much about knowledge but about synonymy. It is enough for me to insist that a description of dispositions provides a revealing elucidation of what it is to know a language, and that the behaviour involved is not mere evidence for such knowledge. As I have said before, to doubt that a person who displays the relevant behaviour knows his language could only be a doubt over the appropriateness of behavioural criteria for a concept of know how, and not over the certainty of inductive inferences from the behaviour to something else.

I can not make much of the argument implied in the first part of the quoted passage. It is true, of course, that what a person will actually say depends on such factors, *inter alia,* as what he had to eat and what his mood might be. And it is true that a definition of 'knowledge of language' which made one man's knowledge differ from another's according to differences in digestion or mood would be a thoroughly bizarre one. Obviously my knowledge of English is not different from yours because I am, and you are not, hungry, so that I do, and you do not, say 'Mm! Delicious' on seeing the *filet mignon.* But when it is said that a person is disposed to behave in certain ways under certain conditions, it is only claimed the behaviour will ensue *ceteris paribus.* What the *ceteris paribus* clause covers will rarely be exhaustively specifiable, and in any particular case, ingenuity and imagination may be required to give even a very rough specification of what is intended to be covered. But this provides no objection against regarding language dispositionally. One may as well object to regarding elasticity as a disposition on the ground that there are innumerable circumstances, unspecifiable in advance, which would prevent an elastic body from stretching under the conditions stated in the conditional. Obviously we can hold that two bits of rubber are equally elastic despite the fact that their histories of stretching vary greatly — because, say, one of the bits was much hotter than the other on some occasion, or because it had been coated with a hard-drying paint. Just as we are entitled to, and must, hold equal factors like abnormal heat or coating with paint in describing the bits of rubber as equally elastic, so we are entitled to, and must, hold factors like nutritional level or mood equal in describing men as having the same knowledge of English. Contrary to what Chomsky says, DA will not describe knowledge of language in such a way that it varies according to the factors mentioned, for these are taken care of in the *ceteris paribus* clause. I do not want to suggest there are no problems here; only that these pertain to all dispositions, not linguistic ones in particular. Since we shall not give up all dispositional talk in the face of these well-known problems, we shall not give up DA either.

4). It would be empty, let us grant, to talk of dispositions to verbal behaviour unless it is possible to make at least rough predictions concerning the likelihood of items of behaviour occurring. Chomsky, stressing that this is indeed crucial, then writes:

> But it must be recognized that the notion of 'probability of a sentence' is an entirely useless one, under any known interpretation of this term. On empirical grounds, the probability of my producing some given sentence of English . . . is indistinguishable from the probability of my producing a given sentence in Japanese (1968-9 : p. 57).

This argument has no force whatsoever. One might as well argue against the elasticity of sea-sponges on the ground that the probability of any particular sea-sponge's being stretched by someone is no greater than its remaining unstretched inside a sunken Spanish galleon. The probability of stretching, implied in describing the sponge as elastic, is of course relative to certain conditions. The sponge will probably stretch if someone or something exerts pressure, or whatever. Once conditions are specified, such as that a person has been asked a certain question, the probability of his uttering a certain expression in English will vastly exceed that of his uttering some expression in Japanese.

5). But Chomsky has a counter to the above reply:

> Introduction of the notion of 'probability relative to a situation' changes nothing, at least if situations are characterized on any known objective grounds . . . (1968-9 : p. 57).

He is arguing that DA fails since the verbal behaviour we are allegedly disposed towards is unpredictable even when the conditions thought, by its proponents, to elicit it are specified. Hence reference to dispositions is empty. An example from

Chomsky's review of Skinner's *Verbal Behavior* illustrates his point. Suppose the conditions are those of my having been placed in front of a certain painting. Surely it is impossible to predict what I shall say. I might say 'Dutch', 'Never saw it before', Beautiful', 'I thought you liked abstract work', or just about anything. I make three comments, in increasing order of importance, on this objection:

a). The extent to which the unpredictability of a man's utterance under specified conditions empties content from attributing to him a given disposition will depend on the nature of the disposition in question. Suppose we are concerned with whether a person knows his grammar in so far as being able to form subject-predicate sentences. It is then irrelevant that we do not predict at all exactly just what utterances he will produce. All we need predict is that he will with some frequency produce utterances of the subject-predicate variety. Detailed prediction has no more place than in confirming the bare hypothesis that something has weight by observing it to fall.

b). That an item of behaviour is not one in a range of items we predicted on the basis of a dispositional hypothesis does not preclude it from serving to confirm the hypothesis. On hindsight the item may be regarded as one we could reasonably have included among the predicted alternatives. Indeed, dispositional hypotheses are likely to take the form 'If. . ., then X, Y, or Z, *or* something relevantly like them will take place'. Suppose we have hypothesized that a man is of a very violent disposition, and predict that under provocation he is likely either to smash a chair over the provoker's head, or knife him, or punch him. Suppose, in fact, he throws him out of the window. While this was not an eventuality mentioned amongst our predictions, it is clearly one that does confirm our hypothesis about his violent disposition. Equally, the fact that a person does not employ a word in just the sentence-frames we explicitly predicted, or does not form passives from actives in just the words we expected, need not falsify the hypotheses that he was disposed to behaviour displaying his knowledge of the word's meaning or of how to form passives.

135

c). Chomsky takes a remarkably meagre view, which he foists upon DA, of the eliciting conditions relevant in determining whether a person is disposed to a certain kind of behaviour. One can readily grant that if the only eliciting conditions were like the mere being-put-in-front-of-a-picture variety, little enough could be predicted about a man's utterances even under specified conditions. But no one viewing language as a complex of dispositions is going to regard such conditions as a very important, let alone the sole, type. Most crucially of all, Chomsky ignores the roles that utterances themselves will play in eliciting verbal behaviour. If we add to the bare situation of putting a man in front of a painting such ingredients as instructing him what to say about it (e.g. to describe its colour), or asking him questions about it, the predictability of what he will say is vastly increased. Questioning — especially of a kind that demands the subject's assent to or dissent from some proposition — is particularly important. Presumably there is no one surer way of ascertaining that a man knows what 'It is raining' means than to get him, on both wet and dry days, to answer the question 'Is it raining?'. For another thing, questioning may be the only way in which we can distinguish between a person whose quirkish and unsolicited utterances betoken merely a quirkish mind, and a person whose quirkish and unsolicited utterances betray a real lack of linguistic knowledge. A man whose everyday utterances are odd may simply be an odd man, whose genuine knowledge of the language will, however, be displayed when he is forced to give appropriate answers to our questions. Or he may be a man whose utterances are odd because he does not understand what he is saying — and our questioning should reveal that too. It is for reasons like this that I said (p. 129) performance factors must be crucial in ascertaining competence. Appropriate performance in context, of a type Chomsky officially regards as irrelevant to competence, is essential to it. Appropriate performance under interrogation in particular is the acid test of competence.

The usual objections levelled against DA, then, are unconvincing. I want to spend a little time mentioning some of its merits; merits which reside, I think, not so much in what the account contains as in what it omits. Indeed, I imagine it is the case with dispositional analyses in general — of, say, motives or beliefs — that their merits, if any, consist in being parsimonious accounts unadorned by the riches, but also unencumbered by the embarrassments, of alternative analyses.

Someone will say, no doubt, that DA omits too much. Does it really explain anything? Does it tell us anything we did not know already? Well, I do not know if it tells us anything new. I have never claimed it is an exciting account. As for the charge that it explains nothing, I am not sure what it amounts to. DA does explain what knowledge of language is. If it is meant that its predictive powers are slight, the reply is that DA, conjoined with a grammar for the language, has just the predictive power of KLT. For wherever

> . . . we might account for a person's competence by appeal to his knowledge of certain principles, in every case we need assume only that the person in question knows how to do something in accordance with the relevant principles (Harman 1968-9b : p. 427).

For example, whatever could be predicted on the assumption that a speaker has non-trivial, unconscious knowledge of rule R could be predicted on the assumption that he follows$_2$ R (on the harmless of the views of rule-following$_2$ described in chapter 3).

What is 'left out', it might be said, is any mention of the 'categorical' states which underly and result in dispositions. In fact it is a general criticism made of dispositional analyses that they allow the possibility of two things being identical in all respects other than their dispositional characteristics.[5] Certainly it would be peculiar to think there might be two objects like this, though I doubt that it is absurd. At any rate, the claim that linguistic knowledge is a complex of dispositions is not meant to exclude the strong likelihood that underlying these dispositions are 'categorical' states common to all persons with similar knowledge. To grant this, though, is not to grant that the 'cateogrical' states consist in states of non-trivial, unconscious knowledge of the type proposed by KLT — as distinct from, say, states of the central nervous system. Such states, as we saw in chapter 4, are not to be described as knowledge even if 'functionally equivalent' to possible states of knowledge.

The most obvious merit of DA is its omission of any reference to unconscious knowledge, 'internalization' of rules, 'mental representations' of structures, and the like. Slightly less obviously, it avoids any implausible model of performance of the type that is necessary in KLT (see pp. 49ff). If unconscious knowledge of rules, structures, and so on, partially explains linguistic performance — and surely it must be thought to if it is identified with knowing a language — then it could only be through the role it plays in some causal mechanism. Performance will result, partly, from consultation of, selection of, and application of rules and principles the speaker unconsciously knows. Katz makes this model pretty explicit:

> The speaker, for reasons that are biographically but not linguistically relevant, chooses some message he wants to convey to the hearer. . . . The speaker then uses the sentence production procedure to obtain an abstract syntactic structure. . . . After he has a suitable syntactic structure, the speaker utilizes the phonological component of his linguistic description to produce a phonetic shape for it (1967 : p. 88).

The hearer, it is then explained, goes through the reverse process in retrieving the speaker's message. In addition to the crippling difficulties encountered by this model which have already been presented, one might mention the difficulty of understanding what it is to 'choose some message', where this is not the decision to utter certain words, out of various alternatives, but the formulation of what has yet to take *any* linguistic or symbolic form. Or one may wonder what on earth it is the hearer is supposed to retrieve, what it is that he decodes the sentence into (which cannot, on pain of a regress on the proferred account, itself be a sentence). I leave those who adopt the model to resolve these difficulties.[6]

My immediate interest is not in stressing these, and repeating other, problems, but in drawing attention to a shaky

presupposition that likely lurks behind the model of performance in question — a presupposition which has no place in DA,
to its credit. The presupposition is, simply, that any skilled
behaviour, any know how, requires explanation in terms of the
agents' further knowledge of guiding rules, principles, or
whatnot. There is a well-known line of argument against such
a presupposition, beginning with Ryle's dismissal of what he
calls the 'intellectualist legend' (pp. 28ff). There he urged
that not all intelligent behaviour can require explanation
in terms of using and applying rules and principles, since
using and applying them are themselves intelligent activities
which, according to the legend, would therefore require
explanation in terms of further rules and principles — and so
on *ad infinitum*. There is no need for the point to be restricted
to intelligent, in the sense of well-executed, behaviour.[7]
Malcolm, in fact, has extended the point into just the area
that interests us. Writing in connection with the view that
linguistic performance must be explained by a person's grasp
and utilization of a theory of grammatical structure, he
says:

> If the presence of a structure system is supposed to explain
> these abilities and performance, then we need to ask,
> *How* does the person know how to employ the system? Does
> he have another system that shows him how to use this one?
> Or does he *just know* how to use it? But if this latter is
> a rational possibility, then it is also a rational possibility
> that there is *no* structure or system that accounts for
> language mastery, or for any repertoire of skills, abilities,
> or performances. The presence of a guidance system cannot
> be a general requirement for knowledge (pp. 391-2).

Naturally, one would not want to use the fact that not all
performances can be explained by grasping and utilizing rules
or systems as an argument for never explaining some performances in this way. Where a person's behaviour deviates from
what we expected in a sufficiently impressive way, we might
well search for just such an explanation. The person who knew
no English yesterday but who today utters some well-formed
English sentences has, we find out, sat up with a grammar

book and a dictionary overnight which he is now using to 'guide' his utterances. But in the absence of such special circumstances, the fact that we indeed embark upon a regress by insisting that all performances are to be explained by 'guidance' systems is a powerful reason for not supposing that normal linguistic behaviour is to be so explained. Further, of course, our foreigner's guidance by the books he read overnight is not beset with the difficulties that a fluent speaker's guidance by an unconsciously internalized grammar would be.

DA, it scarcely needs mentioning, is not saddled with such an implausible model of performance. By that account performance is related to knowledge in the way that any behaviour is related to behavioural dispositions. There is no assumption of 'guiding' mechanisms bringing about the behaviour.

It is worth noting, at this stage, that a regress argument, not dissimilar to the one just mentioned, can be deployed against the notion of competence found in Chomsky and other proponents of KLT. The argument again serves to discredit a presupposition that may well underlie the notion. Discussing Chomsky's view that knowledge of a language consists in an 'internalization' of a grammar, or 'an internal representation of a system of rules', Harman writes:

> Taken literally, he would be saying that we are to explain how it is that Smith knows how to speak and understand a language by citing his knowledge of another more basic language in which he has (unconsciously) 'internally represented' the rules of the first language. . . . The main problem with such a literal interpretation of these remarks would be the implausibility of the resulting view. How, for example, would Smith understand the more basic language? In order to avoid either an infinite regress or a vicious circle, one would have to suppose that Smith can understand at least one language directly, without unconsciously knowing the rules for that language. But if this is admitted, there is no reason why Smith cannot know directly the language he speaks (1967 : p. 76).

The point is that the presupposition lurking, engendered

perhaps by reflection on how we understand a foreign language, to the effect that understanding a language must depend upon possession of another system in terms of which we may interpret it, leads to a regress. Harman's eminently reasonable point seems to have been totally misunderstood by his critics. Arbini, for example, takes the suggestion that Smith might know his language 'directly' as meaning Smith might know it without having learned it — a possibility he rightly rejects. But Harman means Smith could know his language 'directly' in the sense of not understanding it on the basis of some internalized rule system. Arbini's point is relevant, therefore, only if one quite unreasonably takes learning to necessarily involve such unconscious internalization. Again, Chomsky thinks it pertinent to reply that there is no circle or regress in imagining a computer which 'speaks' a language as a result of having been programmed with rules (1969b : p. 156). But it is not. Harman is not denying that it may sometimes be necessary to explain a grasp of one language in terms of a previous grasp of another, which one uses to interpret the former. This is just what we would do, in fact, in the case of learning a second language. He is denying only that it could always be necessary, and insisting presumably that we should only do so where there are special reasons. Now there may be special reasons in the case of the computer (assuming, which is dubious, that we want to talk about computers in these ways) for explaining its 'speech' by a programme represented in a different, 'computerese language'. But this will have no bearing on whether the linguistic ability of the fluent speaker is to be similarly explained.

I said earlier that the merits of DA consist mainly in what it omits. What I meant, I can now say, is not so much the omission of incoherent and implausible claims which figure in the platform of KLT, but of the rather general presuppositions which might have played a role in generating these and like claims.[8] DA can perhaps be seen as deriving from the realization that these presuppositions about how performance is to be explained, or how competence is to be conceived, contain the seeds of infinite regress; as a determination not to embark upon even the first step of such a regress.

So DA is a correct, albeit dull, account of what knowing a language is. Having said something to defend the claim that it is correct, let me say something to defend the claim that it is dull. It is dull because I do not intend to contrast it with some of the views that dispositionalists often wish to contrast their analyses with. Hence I do not make it specific enough to be over-controversial. That would be a task for another book. Dispositional accounts of meaning, for example, are sometimes taken to contrast with accounts in terms of speakers' intentions[9], or of conventions.[10] I do not want DA to contrast with such accounts. On the contrary, I am pretty sure that understanding what was meant by a sentence, and ultimately what a sentence means, has something to do with recognizing speakers' intentions. But I see no reason why such recognition — or, at any rate, its overt manifestations — should not be included in the behaviour towards which we are disposed by our knowledge of a language. I am pretty sure, too, that understanding meanings has something to do with understanding various conventions for their employment — where conventions are interpreted in Lewis' way as a regular pattern of reciprocal beliefs and expectations. But again, I see no reason to exclude such beliefs and expectations, or their overt manifestations, from the behaviour countenanced by DA.

Notes to chapter 7

1   For example Harman (1967 : 1968-9b).
2   Smart, for example, insists on this.
3   For example Slobin and Fodor (1966).
4   See McNeill (1970) and Slobin.
5   Armstrong, for instance, criticizes dispositional analyses of psychological terms along these lines.
6   See Harman (1968) and Wheatley, who both draw attention to this problem.
7   Hence I doubt the relevance of Fodor's (1968b) reply to Ryle, which consists in pointing out that everyday linguistic behaviour

is not intelligent in this sense and so not subject to Ryle's argument.

8   I say 'rather general presuppositions' since I suspect they play a role in several well-known psychological theories; for example, in Piaget's cognitive theory. His 'schemata' appear to be 'guiding' systems. See also Schwartz's review of Bruner et. al. *Studies in Cognitive Growth,* in this connection.

9   By Bloomfield for instance.

10   By Ziff 1966 for instance.

Chapter 8

Words and Concepts

I have said relatively little about semantic knowledge so far, mainly because the doctrines being assessed have stemmed primarily from reflections on the form of the syntactic component in grammar. True, certain rather obvious facts about meaning were important in suggesting to transformational grammarians the form this component should take, but KLT is first and foremost a doctrine about the kind of knowledge underlying our ability to form, and make judgments about, syntactically well-formed sentences. In so far as a theory of semantic knowledge has been developed by grammarians, the focus has been upon sentential meanings — upon, say, the 'projection rules' speakers are utilizing to derive semantic readings for sentences. Remarkably little has been said, therefore, about the meanings, and about our knowledge of the meanings, of individual words — about what we might call 'lexical knowledge'. Still, views about lexical knowledge have emerged in very recent writings of proponents of KLT, though they are, in general form, quite traditional ones. It is important for me to consider the issue of lexical knowledge, apart from the intrinsic interest of it, and apart from the fact that no book ignoring it could respectably be called something like 'Knowledge of Language'. For the views I have in mind would seem to conflict with the little I said about lexical knowledge in the previous chapter — to the effect that knowing a word's meaning is a disposition to behave (in the liberal sense of behaviour allowed). Furthermore these views contain a strong 'innatist' element; hence examination of them is part of an examination of the new innateness hypothesis, which is one of the stated aims of this book. Indeed, it is upon the 'innatist' element that I shall focus.

I will call the collection of views I have in mind the 'Conceptual Thesis' (CT). The first of the views is that knowing the meaning of a word is to be elucidated in terms of knowing or having the concept which it (or some expressions containing it) express, denote, name, or whatever. The second of the views is that coming to know the meanings of any words requires prior knowledge of certain innate, or at any rate native (see p. 3), concepts. The two views are not unrelated. If it is held that a person knows what a word means through discovering what concept it expresses, then it seems some concepts must be known prior to the development of language; otherwise he would have no concepts in terms of which to understand his first words, no way of telling what they mean. I cannot understand what 'bottle' means unless I know what it is to be a bottle, unless I have the concept of *bottle.* So, unless I know what certain things are — unless I already have certain concepts — I cannot come to understand what any word means. Further argument would be needed, naturally, to show that these prelinguistic concepts were innate or 'native'. But since the innateness hypothesis necessarily rests on the view that some concepts are held prelinguistically, it will be enough to discredit that view in order to refute the innateness hypothesis.

It will help if we give CT some owners, and illustrate and elaborate it with some representative quotes. For Katz, the meaning of a word can be displayed in a 'dictionary entry', composed (mainly) of so-called 'semantic markers', each of which 'must stand for parts of senses, or as we shall say, *concepts* out of which senses are composed' (1972 : p. 100f). For example, a set of semantic markers for one sense of 'bachelor' will be:

(Object), (Physical), (Human), (Adult), (Male), (Not married) This provides the information, *inter alia,* that 'a conceptual component of the sense of 'bachelor' is the concept of being a physical object (as opposed to a perceptual object)' (p. 102). There is no doubt that, for Katz, a person who knows the meaning of a word knows, in some sense, the concepts it (or rather its set of semantic markers) expresses — for a person's 'semantic competence' includes at least 'the dictionary information he has' (p. 103). Katz seems to conceive of concepts as objects of some sort, though not as purely psychological objects like wishes or fears. In fact he explains their status as being like Frege's 'Gedanken'. Like theorems, concepts exist whether or not anyone discovers them, though a person who does discover one has succeeded in representing an 'imperfect facsimile' of it to himself (p. 122).

It is pretty clear, too, that Katz would subscribe to the 'innatist' view in CT. But for an explicit statement of this we can turn to Vendler's recent book *Res Cogitans*. For Vendler as for Katz knowing a word's meaning is knowing the concept(s) it expresses.[1] He then raises the problem of how a child learns his first language.

> . . . we have found that the learning of a word, as a meaningful element . . . presupposes the existence of a framework of thought (including a grasp of concepts (D.E.C.)) . . . the most reasonable explanation is that a child must learn his native tongue in a way similar to the way one learns a second language. He must have, in other words, a native equipment that codes the fundamental illocutionary, syntactic, and semantic features of any possible human language. . . . It makes sense, therefore, to speak of one basic conceptual framework, which is the matrix underlying the various natural languages. . . . Learning a word, for the child, is like fitting a stone into the appropriate place in the mosaic (p. 139f).

He then makes 'educated guesses' as to what the 'native stock of concepts' might include — and lists among others the concepts of *person, object, state, change, purpose, causation, time, extension* and *number*. He does not, as far as I can tell, go into the question of these concepts' ontological status. But when he remarks that they are 'universal' and 'intersubjective' I take it he may well be siding with Katz's allegedly Fregean interpretation.

I do not find the notion(s) of concept being employed

by Katz and Vendler at all clear, though I do think it is clear that they cannot be employing certain notions. There is, for example, a perfectly harmless way of treating the expression 'having a concept' in which no one could object to equating having a concept with knowing a word's meaning. In this sense, 'having a concept' is simply defined, stipulatively, as 'knowing a meaning'. I have no doubt that many writers who talk of people having concepts intend to say no more than that they know what various words mean. But Katz and Vendler cannot be intending this trivial sense. For one thing, nothing could be elucidated or explained about knowledge of meaning by appealing to possession of concepts in this sense. Nor would the talk of concepts as objects with which we may be acquainted, or of which we may form imperfect facsimiles, be warranted by this sense. For such talk is controversial, and nothing of a controversial type could be inferred from the fact that people have concepts in no more exciting a sense than that they know what certain words mean.

There is another notion of having a concept, favoured by psychologists, in which it is equated with certain classificatory or discriminatory abilities. John Carroll, for example, writes:

> ... when the child will accept and make a common response to any one of a number of rather different stimuli — for example, any one of a number of different foods — ... he has attained the concept of 'food' in some elementary sense (p. 78).

But not only is this notion explicitly rejected by Vendler, it is one that would make nonsense of the reference to concepts as objects. Nor could people be forming 'mental representations' or 'imperfect facsimiles' of concepts in the sense of discriminatory abilities. Nor could they be 'intersubjective' — or 'subjective' either.

So while I am not clear just what notion of having a concept is at work in CT, it is relatively clear what ones are not. And I think it is enough for our purposes that, without knowing just what is being said, CT is saying *at least:*

    i).   to have a concept is to be acquainted, in some manner, with an object.

ii). knowing the meanings of words is elucidated as having concepts, and this knowledge is distinct from and explanatory of the know how a person exhibits in his speech behaviour.

iii). a person's linguistic behaviour is at best good empirical evidence for his lexical knowledge; for, that is, his having the relevant concepts.

iv). some concepts must be possessed before the meaning of any words at all can be understood.

Certainly CT is very much in the spirit of KLT. The knowledge postulated by both theses is, typically, 'unconscious' or 'implicit'; and in both cases it is supposed to explain the know how exhibited in behaviour — whether it be knowing how to employ a particular word, or knowing how to form synatactically acceptable sentences. Further, CT shares with KLT an 'innatist', or at any rate a 'nativist', ingredient. Indeed, the innate concepts of CT would seem to have far more in common with the innate ideas of 17th & 18th C. rationalism than the syntactic categories, structures, and principles of KLT would. Perhaps it is Vendler, with his 'native stock of concepts', more than Chomsky, who is truly rekindling the older rationalism.

Each element ((i) — iv)) in CT has been the target of criticism over the years. At any rate, views which are obvious ancestors of CT have been intensely criticized.[2] Danto remarks that philosophical reputations have grown fat on just such criticisms. I shall take a somewhat different tack, partly because these earlier criticisms are well-known, and partly because they have obviously failed to convince in all circles.

It is upon the 'innatist' ingredient that I shall focus, though the points raised against it will carry over against the more general position of CT. The totally effective way to show that conceptual knowledge is not required prior to the development of semantic abilities would be to show that, even when such abilities *have* developed, there is still no conceptual knowledge of the type supposed. If we find it false or absurd to attribute concepts to children who have come of linguistic age, we shall hardly find it less false or absurd to attribute them to children who have not. And this is just what I intend to show.[3]

Let us consider, then, children of between the ages, roughly, of 1½ to 3 years; those in the infancy of speech. The speech of these children is sometimes referred to as 'telegraphic'. This metaphor — which I shall later suggest is misleading '— is designed to stress that not only are their sentences very short, but that they typically omit just the sorts of words that an adult might omit for economic reasons from his telegrams; pronouns, for example, or parts of the verb 'to be'. In fact, I shall define 'young children', for my purposes, as those whose speech lacks a certain 'logico-syntactic apparatus'. I explicate this notion ostensively: it is an apparatus which includes at least the following elements — articles, plurals, pronouns, identity operators, and quantifiers. It may be that no flesh-and-blood children are young children in the defined sense, since the speech of a randomly selected child will probably not totally lack occurrences of at least some of the elements mentioned. To that extent, my young children are models — but models to which actual children, especially the very young ones, approximate quite closely.

It is generally and traditionally assumed — especially by mothers and child psychologists — that young children possess a reasonably rich stock of concepts. Depending on the child's experience, he may be expected to have such concepts as *dog, father, doll, red,* or *food,* as well as more 'abstract-sounding' ones like *self, similarity,* or *action.* This is sometimes qualified by adding that his concepts are 'embryonic' or 'elementary', on the ground perhaps that he is unable to give any description of them, or in a Piagetian vein, that he can only employ them in 'concrete' as opposed to 'formal' thought-operations. Still, it is assumed that even if the child is not yet Ryle's 'le penseur', his stock of concepts is sizeable.

It is this traditional assumption I intend, in the first instance, to challenge. The young child does not have an embryonic concept of, say, *dog;* he has no such concept at all. What encourages the traditional assumption is, without doubt, the fact that children make noises which are phonetically similar to ones made by adults when speaking; a fact which encourages the view that the children are uttering the same words, with the same meanings, as their elders. But this view is over-hasty. It would be wiser to approach the young child's speech in the spirit of a translator encountering a hitherto untranslated language; and it would be a rash translator who assumed that foreign noises phonetically similar to ones made by Englishmen were therefore utterances of English words. The Slav who makes the noise /bled/ is probably referring to a town in northern Yugoslavia, and not uttering the past tense of 'to bleed'. Of course, it is not this fact alone which encourages the traditional assumption. In addition there is the fact that we are able to provide pragmatically adequate interpretations of the child's noises. I mean for example that if we treat the child's /dǫg/ or /dǫ . gi/ as if it meant what adults mean by the word 'dog', we can, within limits, successfully predict when the child will make that noise, and what his responses on hearing it will be. This encourages us to think the child is therefore using and understanding the word 'dog', and so has the concept of dog. But we should resist thinking this.

Suppose we note that the noise /ʃjẽ/ (/chien/) occurs fairly frequently in little Pierre's two or three word utterances, and that by interpreting it as an utterance of a word having the meaning in French of our word 'dog', we are able to predict Pierre's employment of it and his responses to it. What more, it might be asked, is required to vindicate treating his noise as 'chien', and as meaning what 'dog' means? Well, a whole lot more is required.

Our word 'dog', remember, is a noun, and a noun of a certain sort. It is concrete and general. Hence it is to be distinguished from words which are not nouns at all, and from abstract nouns, proper nouns, mass nouns, and so on. Suppose now we were to treat Pierre's 'chien' as an adjective ('doggish' perhaps) which expresses a property things have. Or suppose we translate it as an abstract noun ('doghood' perhaps) which names an abstract entity that Fido, Bonzo, and Cerberus instantiate. Or as a mass noun ('dogium' perhaps) which names the stuff out of which Fido and his friends are composed. A little reflection would reveal that these alternative translations, when accompanied by suitable translations of the words, if any, which accompany 'chien' in Pierre's utterances, will all have equal pragmatic adequacy. If we interpret a remark of his to mean 'Here is another lump of dogium' instead of 'Here is another dog', we shall be equally able to predict when he is likely to make it — when, say, Fido comes into the room shortly after Bonzo. Pierre's appropriate response to a maternal command is just as well accounted for by supposing he interprets it to mean 'Look for your favourite doggish object' as by supposing he interprets it as 'Look for your favourite dog'. Either way he sets off in search of Cerberus, or the hound of the Baskervilles.

It is immaterial, of course, that Pierre is French. Just as alternative treatments of his /ʃjẽ/ could all be pragmatically adequate, so could alternative treatments of little Peter's /dǫ . gi/. Now since the only evidence we have to go on is the child's overt behaviour, and since this is neutral as between the various translations, it follows that any particular translation we give goes beyond anything the evidence could possibly determine. This is done, for example, when McNeill, in connection with a 12-month old girl who began to utter /hɒt/ in the presence of things not at that moment hot, claims:

> The child showed that 'hot' was not merely the label of hot objects, but was also said of objects that could be hot. It asserted a property (1970 : p. 24).

One might just as well speculate that the child's 'hot' was the name of objects that could be hot; or the name of the stuff out of which frequently hot things are composed; or the name of the sensation that various objects reminded her of — and so on.

The point, at the level of concepts, will be this: to provide the various different translations of the child's words will be to attribute to him quite different concepts. This will be so, at any rate, if, as by CT, one takes there to be some intimate connection between employing a word with a certain meaning and having a certain concept. For instance, to have the concept of *dog* is, as Katz would stress, to have a certain physical object concept. To have the concept of a stuff out of which' the objects are composed would be to have a quite different one. To have that of a property belonging to the objects would be to have a third.[4] In so far as we waver between different translations of Pierre's or Peter's words, we waver between attributing to them quite different concepts. Yet just as the choice of translation is not determined by the only available evidence, nor will the attribution of a particular concept.

It is essential to realize that we would not be faced with the variety of translations and concept-attributions if the children employed, and we could identify in their speech, the sort of logico-syntactic apparatus mentioned earlier — articles, plurals, copulas, quantifiers, etc.. This is because the differences between a word translatable as 'dog' and ones translatable as 'dogium', 'doghood', or whatever, would be revealed within such an apparatus. Our concrete, general noun 'dog' is distinguished from other words (adjectives, abstract nouns, mass nouns, and so on) by, *inter alia,* taking articles, being pluralizable, being replaceable by pronouns or bound variables in distinctive ways, occurring in certain kinds of identity statements, and so on. So, if we could identify such elements in the child's speech, then we would be in a position to tell which of the various translations to give his words, and hence which of the various concepts to attribute to him.

The trouble is that this is just what we *cannot* do in the case of young children, who have been defined as those whose speech lacks elements from precisely such an apparatus. Even if actual children sometimes employ some of the elements, or rather employ sounds phonetically similar to those we make in using these elements, they do not do so with sufficient frequency, consistency, or sophistication for us to accurately identify and interpret them. For example, if we knew that the final '-s' in Peter's 'doggies' was a pluralization, we could say that his 'doggie' was our 'dog', and not 'dogium', 'doggish', or 'doghood', since these latter do not take plurals. But there is no good reason to take his final '-s' in this way. We might, instead, suppose it functions like our expressions 'collection of' or 'bits of', in which case we could stick to translating 'doggie' as 'dogium'. Where we say 'There is a dog',

Peter is saying, as it were, 'Here is a bit of dogium'; and where we say 'There are some dogs', Peter is saying 'There are some bits of dogium'. It is not until Peter uses the final '-s' with considerable frequency and consistency that we shall be warranted in taking it as our plural ending.[5]

It might, I suppose, be argued that the child does employ the logico-syntactic apparatus; it is just that its elements do not receive vocalic expression in the child's speech. We encountered a suggestion along these lines in chapter 3 (p. 41), when we were guarding against exaggerration of the role of rules in language, particularly children's language. McNeill had argued that while the child may rarely voice /iz/, this does not mean he is not using the copula; rather he is following a 'rule' that allows him to delete the copula from the vocalized utterance. Certainly psycholinguists who take children's words to be determinately translatable are well-advised to adopt such a position, for by doing so they concede that words are only translatable within a logico-syntactic structure. The trouble is I see no reason to accept this position, or suggestions like McNeill's. Of course, if we assume that the child's speech is just like adult speech, only *telegraphic,* then we shall generously read into the child's utterances the missing, unvocalized elements — just as we read into our adult friend's telegram the words he could not afford to pay for. But I am entitled to do this in the case of my friend because I know his sentences are not normally truncated in the way his telegram is. I have no similar warrant, though, for reading words into the child's short sentences. 'Truncated' speech, for the child, is the norm. For this reason, I find the metaphor of tele-graphic speech seriously misleading.

I may have given the impression that the problem is simply one of our not *knowing* the correct translations to give, or the actual concepts to ascribe, because of insufficient evidence. If so, let me correct that impression. The real point is that it makes no sense to talk of one out of a number of pragmatically adequate translations being the correct one, or of one out of the corresponding concepts being the proper one to ascribe. The logico-syntactic apparatus which the child does not employ serves not to furnish extra evidence but to provide the very criteria in terms of which correct translation can be distinguished from incorrect; in terms of which kinds of words can be distinguished, along with the corresponding kinds of concepts expressed by them. A word is our word 'dog' precisely by virtue of the fact, *inter alia,* that it occurs in specific ways within such an apparatus. And the concept of *dog* is the concept it is because of the way words expressing it occur within the apparatus. Having identified what kind of word it is, or what kind of concept it is, we can go on to ask whether we have translated or ascribed correctly. Should it have been translated as 'pup' rather than 'dog'? Did he have the concept of *dog* or of *pup*? But not before. Put crudely, to employ the word 'dog' in its usual meaning *is* to employ it in distinctive ways within the apparatus.[6] Perhaps an analogy will help. It makes no sense to ask of a practice in a society which has no machinery for promulgating, recognizing, or enforcing laws whether it is legal or illegal — not because we lack sufficient evidence, but because there is nothing to judge. Equally, we cannot judge, rightly or wrongly, the correct translation of words that do not occur within the relevant apparatus, for there is no way of telling what kinds of words they, or the concepts expressed, might be. There is, in fact, nothing to judge.[7]

But what has this to do with CT — either with the general view that lexical knowledge is to be explained in terms of having concepts, or the 'innatist' view that no meanings can be learned without prior grasp of at least some concepts? For, in connection with the latter view, might not a proponent of CT reply:

> We grant that it is impossible to give determinate translations of a young child's words. But this does not contradict the claim that he must possess certain concepts before he can know what his words mean — before, that is, his words become determinately translatable. To show this, you would have to produce a child who *does* use words with determinate meanings but who never had a prior grasp of any concepts. And your young children are not like that.

But this reply ignores the *reasons* I gave for not crediting children with particular meanings, or knowledge of these. The basic point was that until the words are used within a certain apparatus, there can be no telling what kinds of words they are, or what kinds of concepts they express. There was no way of telling, for instance, whether 'doggie' was a physical object word, a property word, a stuff word, or what. Prior to the emergence of the apparatus, therefore, there is no sense in supposing that a word has, as part of its meaning, the expression of a concept like *physical object,* or *stuff.* But if the child does not have these concepts prior to the emergence of a certain, rather sophisticated linguistic apparatus then, *ipso facto,* he does not have them prior to his coming to have some understanding of language. Yet these are just the sort of concepts which, according to Vendler and others, are part of the 'native stock' which must be grasped if any language is to be learned at all. They must, we see, be wrong. The identification of concept-possession is impossible in the absence not merely of some linguistic abilities, but relatively sophisticated abilities.

There is a harmless way of interpreting the claim that before a child can understand what words mean, he must grasp certain concepts. We do this by depriving 'before' of any temporal sense — as we do in 'Before we can call him a bachelor, he must be unmarried'. But this interpretation will not allow any psychological conclusions of a 'nativist' sort to be drawn. Indeed, the resulting claim will be one that a person who has stipulatively equated 'knowing a meaning' and 'having a concept' can happily accept. For such a definition will guarantee that before (timeless sense) one knows a meaning one must have a concept. Further, this is an interpretation that Katz and Vendler cannot be intending. Vendler, remember, compares learning a first language on the basis of a 'native code' with learning a second language on the basis of a first — and, here, there is clearly a temporal direction involved.

Even if the proponent of CT is willing, by dropping any temporal content from 'Before a child can know meanings, he must have concepts', to give up the 'innatist' or 'nativist' ingredient, he may see no reason to give up the more general view contained in CT. Indeed, he may see, in the joint impossibility of either identifying meanings or identifying concepts in young children's speech, support for the view that having concepts explains knowing meanings. But again, this will ignore the reasons I have for thinking it impossible to identify meanings or concepts in the child's speech.

First: if having a concept is to be more than barely synonymous with knowing a meaning, in such a way that the former can be used to elucidate the latter, then it must be conceivable that a person should have the concept without employing or knowing the meanings of any words that happen to express that concept — in a way that it is not conceivable to know the meanings without having the concept. If, say, the concept is some object, or a Lockean general idea, one could surely have it without having any words that name or express it. If this is denied, I simply do not see how having the concept could count as more basic than, and as explanatory of, knowing word meanings. Anyway, the conceivability of this situation is explicitly admitted by Vendler:

> As the same word can be encoded in spoken or written symbols, the same concept, and the same thought, can be encoded in the various languages *and* in the 'code', as yet unknown, operating in the human nervous system (p. 142).

Presumably it follows that a concept might be 'encoded' only in the 'code' of the nervous system, and not in any verbal one. Yet the *possibility,* and not just the actuality, of there being identifiable concepts possessed in the absence of a sophisticated logico-syntactic language is ruled out by my arguments. Whatever Vendler's 'code' in the nervous system is supposed to be like, it does not contain articles, plurals, quantifiers, and the like, and is therefore not a code in any sense that could allow us to identify its owners' concepts. Like Goodman

> I know what an embodied idea is — an idea couched in words or other symbols — it does not follow that I know what a disembodied idea is. I know what a horse with spirit is, but not what the spirit is without the horse (1969 : p. 140).[8]

A second point to make about concepts conceived of as objects, acquaintance with which explains lexical knowledge, is the one Quine has made about propositions and the 'uncritical mentalistic theory of ideas' (1960 : p. 74). If there were these concepts, propositions, or ideas, translation between languages would be determinate, which it is not.[9] In the present context, the point would run: if knowing the meaning of a word is having the corresponding concept then even though *we* might be unable to tell what a young child means by a word, there will be a true description to be given of what is meant, and the child will know what he means at any rate. For either he has the corresponding concept or he does not — either, that is, he is acquainted with the right concept or idea, or he is not. If he is, he knows what the word really means. If he is not, he thinks it means something else. So, although we may be in no position to choose between 'dog', 'dogium', 'doghood', etc. as the translation of the child's 'doggie', there is a correct choice to be made. But for obvious reasons, I would not find this position intelligible. If I am correct, the absence of a logico-syntactic apparatus puts paid to determinacy of translation, and hence to the doctrine of concepts which implies it.

There is a way, incidentally, of interpreting 'having a concept' which would allow us to hold (a) that young children do have concepts, and (b) that having concepts precedes lexical knowledge. This is if we interpret concept-possession along Carroll's lines (see p. 147). in terms of certain discriminatory and classificatory abilities. To have the concept of *dog* by this view is a matter of grouping Bonzo, Fido, and Cerberus together, and apart from Kitty, Tabby, or Whiskers; and, when language comes along, of calling a number of things by the name 'dog'. I do not find this an illuminating approach to the notion of having a concept; though I will not here repeat arguments I have given elsewhere (1973c). I simply reiterate that this interpretation is not available to Katz and Vendler (see p. 147). Vendler, indeed, spends some time rejecting just such an account, and for the right reasons. For example, being able to sort out the male from the female chicks shows nothing about whether the sorter has the proper concept of *male chick.*

Finally, I should point out that there is no tension between my dismissal of the 'classification/discrimination' view of concept-possession, and my earlier defence of a dispositional account of linguistic knowledge. I am quite free to include considerably more in the behaviour towards which one is disposed than merely calling similar things by the same name, or responding similarly to similar stimuli. In particular I shall want to include the employment of words within a sophisticated logico-syntactic apparatus. It is not my simply calling what barks 'dog' that shows I know the meaning of the word. In addition I must pluralize the word when necessary, replace it by the right pronouns on the right occasions, use it in appropriate ways in identity statements, and so on.

Notes to chapter 8

1   More exactly, 'the linguistic expression of a concept is a sentence frame partly filled by dummy words' (p. 132). For example, it would not be the word 'push' that expresses the relevant concept, but a 'frame' like 'N pushes N'.

2   I take it that criticisms of so-called 'ideational' or 'mentalistic' theories of meaning, to be found in, say, Alston, are criticisms of such ancestors.

3   What follows is largely taken from my article 'Grammar and the possession of concepts'. The arguments owe a clear debt to Quine's thesis of the 'indeterminacy of translation'. Whether he would approve of the extension of that thesis in connection with children's languages, I do not know.

4   I think it is instructive in this connection to think of Wittgenstein's 'pain-patches'. Surely to have the concept of a property belonging to those things, like stinging nettles, which frequently hurt us would be to have a quite different concept of *pain* from the one we actually have.

5   Frequency and consistency must be essential, since otherwise it is not clear why we should not be sceptical about the meanings of our best, adult friend's words. I take it that his employment of these words within an apparatus of frequently and consistently used logico-syntactic elements is the criterion for saying he means the same by his words as I mean by mine. (See Quine 1969 : p. 48f).

6   Richard Pring has pointed out to me that these syntactic considerations cannot suffice to determine what kind of word a word is. Presumably 'electron' behaves, within the apparatus, like 'dog', but we can still question whether, at a certain level, *electron* is an object concept, let alone a physical object concept.

7   Vendler, oddly enough, stresses the importance of syntactic factors in identifying meanings and concepts, without apparently seeing the implication of how we might identify them in the absence of a sophisticated language. I say he stresses the importance of these factors on the grounds that the 'sentence frames' which, for him, express concepts, serve partly to determine the syntactic features of the words (see note 1).

8   Actually I would not necessarily go along with the claim that ideas must be 'couched in words'. Indeed, I am not sure what it means. It is enough for me to claim, more mildly, that ideas could not be identified in the absence of words.

9   Naturally, this claim of Quine's is contentious. I think, in fact, it is less contentious to claim that a young child's language cannot be determinately translated than that a foreign language cannot. For, in the case of the latter, we might find ways of identifying elements in a logico-syntactic apparatus, in which event determinate translation could proceed (see Hintikka); whereas we know there are no such elements to identify in the young child's speech.

Chapter 9

Linguistic Universals

In chapter 1, I suggested two main arguments for innateness can be found among the 'new rationalists'. According to the one, speakers could not have 'interalized' the grammars of their languages unless some of their grammatical knowledge was innate. Such an argument is discredited to the extent that KLT is. According to the other, only an innateness hypothesis can account for the existence of so-called 'linguistic universals'. While, in my view, this second argument has been the less crucial for Chomsky and others, it is still worth considering. In fact, I will not come to any very definite conclusions about the relation between innateness and universals, though I may present them with rather more confidence than I feel. This is partly because the issue, due to the wide variety of alleged universals, is too vast for a single chapter; and partly because it involves many unsettled empirical questions which are beyond my competence to judge. I shall be happy if I can clarify and lend some order to the range of problems at hand; draw attention to the alternative explanations, besides an 'innatist' one, that universals might admit and, finally, offer some admonitory reflections on the search for, and the status of, linguistic universals.

The suggested link between innateness and universality should ring bells. In particular, it recalls the 17th C. debate over innate ideas. For Glanville, acknowledgment by 'all sober mankind' was the hallmark of innate principles; and for Norris, it was 'universality of consent'. Herbert's innate ideas were 'notitiae communes', while Locke's main argument against innate principles was precisely that there are none

160

'to which all mankind gives an universal consent'! It is true, as these quotes suggest, that it was not mere universality that marked innateness for the 17th C. philosophers. It was, in particular, universality of consent or assent. And this element is generally missing from current reflections. Linguistic universals are not, typically, ones which all men are thought to recognize, or assent to the presence of. Still, the idea that what is universal provides some sort of evidence for innate knowledge — or innate something — is common to older and newer views. We will return to the connection between the 17th C. and the present day shortly.

Linguistic universals — those features (with qualifications to come) which belong to all languages, or to Language itself — play a number of roles in recent linguistic and psycholinguistic theory; and we might look at some of these. First, they figure in descriptions of the processes by which children allegedly learn languages; that is, in models of acquisition.

> A theory of linguistic structure that aims for explanatory adequacy incorporates an account of linguistic universals, and it attributes tacit knowledge of these universals to the child. It proposes, then, that the child approaches the data with the presumption that they are drawn from a language of a certain antecedently well-defined type, his problem being to determine which of the (humanly) possible languages is that of the community in which he is placed. Language learning would be impossible unless this were the case (Chomsky 1965 : p. 27).

This role will hardly appeal to us; since we have rejected the idea that any 'internalization' of a grammar takes place, as well as the idea that the learner goes about, as a 'baby scientist', hypothesizing, testing, and selecting theories of language.

Second, linguistic universals have served to provide the *content* of the speaker's alleged innate knowledge. The boy who speaks English did not know the grammar of English innately, as opposed to that of French. If he did we should have to conclude, implausibly, that he would have been in great trouble had his parents moved to Paris when he was very

161

young. What he knows innately, so it is said, are those principles or categories which belong to English, French, Bantu, and every language that he might have learned.

> The hypothesis we suggest . . . is this: the language acquisition device contains, as innate structure, each of the principles stated within the theory of language . . . (including) the linguistic universals which define the form of a linguistic description (Katz 1966 : p. 269).

This role will not appeal to us either. Having rejected 'unconscious' or 'tacit' knowledge of any non-trivial kind in general, we are not going to accept such knowledge when it is supposed to be innate.

It might seem that I could end this chapter here. Do not all the previous arguments imply rejection of innate grammatical knowledge? Well, if the sole concern was with whether linguistic universals could be evidence for innate *knowledge,* I could. But there are other related, and interesting, possibilities. Schwartz (1969), having dismissed something like KLT and its implications for innate knowledge, writes:

> As I see it, the psychologically interesting question is whether the factors that shape the learning of language are specific to language or whether they are general features of the learning apparatus (p. 189).

Nowhere have I denied that coming to know a language must be the result, partly, of innate human make-up. Indeed, it is a tautology that there is *something* about men, unlearned, which makes learning possible. Nor is this anything an empiricist psychologist could reasonably deny. Even the most vigorous of reinforcement theorists would have to concede that conditioning could only operate if people have natural tendencies to find some stimuli more similar to one another than to others. What they have wanted to deny is that this make-up, this *something* about men, which permits language-learning, is anything but the make-up which permits the learning of skills, and forms of behaviour, in general. There is no reason, they would say, to suppose men to be incapable of learning languages very different from any known at present, provided that the environmental and experiential factors which facilitate learning in general were themselves suitably different. The contrary claim is that there are factors in the human make-up of a peculiarly linguistic kind. These are factors which predispose men to learn languages of only certain types and in only certain ways — types and ways which could not be predicted or explained on the basis of any general assumptions about human nature, human learning, or human experience. If, for example, it could be shown that men could not learn logical calculi as first languages — or could only do so with the greatest difficulty — this would not be something predictable on the basis of general learning theory.

Now this debate is an interesting one, whether or not the alleged innate factors are thought to take the form of knowledge or beliefs about principles of language. In so far as the 'innatist' eschews this epistemological talk, and retreats to hypothesizing predispositions to learn, he will be safe from the objections to KLT. Some writers, as we saw in chapter 1, take the talk of innate knowledge to be a merely metaphorical presentation of the essential point which is, for them, the postulation of specifically linguistic innate predispositions. To take such a view, I suggested, is largely .to renounce philosophical interest in the issues — which is not to say that *we* cannot take a philosophical interest in the residual claim about predispositions. Anyway, it is this claim I shall return to in a moment.

There is a third role linguistic universals have been given to play — this time in aiding the linguist's selection of the 'correct' grammar of a language. We saw that a grammar was 'descriptively adequate', for Chomsky, if in addition to generating all and only grammatical sentences it produced structures that 'correspond to the linguistic intuitions of the native speaker' (1965: p. 24). But any number of grammars may be adequate at this level — and the 'correct' one has to be further justified at the level of 'explanatory adequacy'. This means the grammar must be the one speakers have actually 'internalized' on the basis of the 'primary linguistic data' encountered. But the speakers do this, we are told, by comparing the data against hypotheses drawn from humanly possible grammars; from grammars, that is, which incorporate the linguistic universals constraining the nature of grammars.

I may have given the impression in the above paragraph that I understand what is being said — but I do not. At any rate, I do not see how resort to an acquisition model described in terms of measuring data against humanly possible grammars could determine selection of the 'correct' grammar. We can not pick the 'correct' grammar from various alternatives on the grounds that it is the one actually 'internalized' by children — for, remember, it was precisely because there were alternatives that we could not speak of any one having been 'internalized'. If it did make sense to speak of 'internalization', and if we knew which grammar had been 'internalized', this could only be because we already knew what the 'correct' grammar was. Further, each alternative grammar is one the child might have 'internalized', if he could have 'internalized' any. Now *ex hypothesi* each of these will incorporate universal grammar. Hence I find it impossible to see how appealing to universal grammar could help determine the choice between alternative grammars of a language.[2]

The final, and for us at present, the crucial role universals play is in providing an *argument* for specifically linguistic innate factors. The argument is remarkably simple. Such innate factors would provide a possible explanation for the presence in all languages of certain features. And since no rival explanation has any degree of plausibility, then the innateness explanation wins by default. Katz, for example, having rejected explanations in terms of common origin and similarites of language functions, concludes:

> . . . by this process of elimination, the only thing left that can provide the invariant condition that we want to connect with the universal features of language as their causal antecedent is the common innate endowment of human language learners . . . (1966 : p. 273).

It is this 'what else?' argument that will occupy the middle part of the chapter.

But what is a linguistic universal? One might reasonably expect it to be a feature belonging, in a straightforward way, to all languages — but this expectation is disappointed. While linguists do cite such features — 'strong' universals, as I will call them — they also use the term in a much wider way. Consider, say, the sense in which Jakobson's 'distinctive features' (e.g. voicing, nasality, etc.) are universals of phonology. It is not that the sound systems of all languages exhibit each of these features, but rather that each sound system will exhibit some sub-set of these features and no features outside of Jakobson's list. Equally, Chomsky's 'substantive' universals (e.g. Noun, Past Tense, etc.) are not to be found in the grammars for all languages; rather they are a fixed set of categories some sub-set of which will comprise the categories of each grammar. Let us call these 'weak' universals. Other linguists have said that anything is a universal whose description can fill the blanks in the formula

$$(x) ((x \in L) \supset (. . . . x . . . . .)),$$

where L is the class of languages.[3] This allows for the creation of the most curious 'universals'. There is no language, for instance, which both contains 'jolly' and does not contain 'hockeysticks'. Hence it is true of every language that if it contains 'jolly' then it contains 'hockeysticks'. Yet it sounds a joke to regard the 'feature' of containing-'hockeysticks'-if-containing- 'jolly' as a universal of language. The point is not that the antecedent is satisfied by only one language, namely English, for there are some conditionals in which that is the case which are, nonetheless, of significance. (I gather the fact that the only language having lateral clicks also has dental clicks is of considerable phonological interest). The point is, rather, that such a conditional could not support counterfactuals. We would not, that is, want to rule out the possibility that the next language to be invented or discovered will have 'jolly' but not 'hockeysticks'. Finally, some linguists have so weakened the notion of universals so as to include 'the more than chance frequency of distribution of certain characteristics' (Greenberg 1957 : p. 87). So if one comparative construction occurs with more frequency among

165

languages than others, then that construction is a linguistic universal. Let us call these 'very weak' universals.

It is not my aim to criticize these bizarre uses of the term 'universal' — though that is surely what they are — but to examine the connection between universality and innateness. If we hark back to the 17th C. for a moment, we see that for those philosophers nothing less than strong universality could provide support for innateness. For an idea to be innate, it had to be one possessed by all men without exception (excluding, perhaps, imbeciles). If Locke and his opponents were right on this, then it is apparent that some of the universals proclaimed by linguists could not support an innateness claim. Indeed, by involving the admission that these universals are not present without exception, they would be incompatible with that claim. Imagine Locke's reaction if his denial of the innateness of *God* were met with the following replies: 'Well, although the idea of *God* is not found everywhere, it is still universal (and so innate) since it belongs to a stock of ideas out of which the thoughts of all men are composed', or 'Well, the idea of *God* is universal (and so innate) since it crops up with more than chance frequency in men's thought'. Locke, plainly, would treat these replies as admissions of defeat, not defences of the universality and innateness of the idea of *God.*

But were Locke and his opponents right in thinking that strong universality alone could provide support for innateness? I think not. Recall the Frankenstein's monster from chapter 1. I argued that it could know and believe a variety of things despite having had no experiences at all, so that in an intelligible sense its knowledge and beliefs would be innate. Now it would be no objection to this description of the monster to point out that its knowledge is not universally shared. The nature of the monster's creation and behaviour, which makes it possible to refer to its innate knowledge, makes the universality or otherwise of that knowledge irrelevant. I suspect the following considerations might underlie Locke's mistake. If X is an innate characteristic, it belongs to a man by virtue of his nature, not his experience. But a man's nature is his nature as a human being. Hence what belongs to a man innately belongs to him by virtue of his human nature. But human nature is shared by all men. Hence what is innate in one man must be innate in all men. The fallacy here is in thinking that what belongs to something by its nature belongs to it by virtue of that aspect of its nature that it shares with all other things of the same class. But our monster's innate knowledge did not belong to it by virtue of that aspect of its nature which it shared with all other monsters — whatever that would be.

While Locke is wrong to take strong universality as a necessary condition of innateness, it would be equally wrong to conclude that universality of a strongish kind is *in general* irrelevant. We could ignore universality in our monster's case because we had other, special grounds on which to ascribe innate knowledge. But where these grounds are missing — as they are in the real world[4] — it is difficult to see how innateness claims are to be supported except on the basis of universality, of a strongish kind, of certain characteristics. To suppose, for example, that people who learn English are innately predisposed to learn just that language, would create a problem for explaining how young emigrés seem to have no trouble with the language of their adopted country. We should have to assume that the world is so designed that just those people with a predisposition to learn language L find themselves in the country where L is spoken. Now a very weak, or even a weak, universal will not be good enough. That a feature crops up in languages with more than chance frequency (whatever that means) no more calls for an 'innatist' explanation than the more than chance occurrence of electric guitars would call for an explanation in terms of innate predispositions towards electric guitar playing. Even strong universals will not provide the relevant support unless they are of a certain type. I imagine no actual language, not even Welsh, contains words of more than seventy letters, but this is due to rather general physiological and psychological factors. And we could not predict that a future language, spoken by a people whose general vocal apparatus or powers of memory were different from our own, would not contain such words. This means that strong universals can only provide support for specifically linguistic innate factors if they support counter-factuals about possible languages. These we might call 'very strong' universals.

The need for very strong, counterfactual supporting, universals is not always appreciated — though it is by Chomsky, who writes:

> . . . if an artificial language were constructed which violated some of these general principles, then it would not be learned at all, or at least not learned with the ease and efficiency with which the normal child learns human language (quoted in Lyons p. 111).

The trouble is there can be no direct way of testing this argument. Children cannot be made to learn, as first languages, any but actual, natural languages. Certain indirect tests might exist — and these, in fact, seem to militate against Chomsky's argument. After all, children do manage to learn artificial 'languages' at a fairly early age; and before they learn their native language, they have learned various communicative skills, such as making gestures, which do not share some of the 'general principles' of language. But I will not pursue these points. Their relevance can quite reasonably be challenged. The important thing is to see that the only real support for there being very strong universals, and so an innate linguistic factor, can be, first, that there are strong linguistic universals in all actual languages, and second, the difficulty of explaining their presence away in any other terms (in the sort of terms, for example, that we explained away the universal absence of seventy letter words).

While universals capable of supporting 'innatist' claims must be very strong, counterfactual supporting ones, they need not — paradoxical though it may sound, and in retraction of what I have just said — actually be *strong* ones. I mean that the absence of some very widespread feature from one or a few languages need not, by itself, falsify the claim that this feature reflects an innate linguistic factor, or the claim that possible languages lacking it would be impossible or very difficult to learn. Even Locke allowed that the imbecile's lack of an idea would not show that the idea was not innate.

The essential requirement is not that each language should contain the feature but that, if any do not, there is a good explanation of why not. The feature's presence could be law-like provided that its occasional absence is explicable in terms of irregularities in the conditions under which the laws operate. In that case, the near universality of the feature could still warrant counterfactual statements.[5] For an earlier view, what is innate is implanted by God, and for a more contemporary view the result of evolutionary neurological development. Well, God might have left some people out of his seeding, and normal development might have been hindered in some cases. Provided we are able to guess at God's or Nature's little foibles, this will not matter in connection with innateness.

The case for innateness, then, will depend on there being very strong linguistic universals, and on the impossibility of accounting for these in alternative ways. I shall begin with the latter. It would be nice to plunge in at once, but this cannot be done until it is appreciated how great the variety of alleged universals is. There will be no reason to think a single overall explanation will be applicable in each case. Hence, one does not refute the innateness hypothesis by showing, in certain cases, that other explanations are more plausible. But neither will one establish the hypothesis by showing that there is no single alternative which could account for all universals. The following list of some alleged universals give some idea of the variety:

    i.   All languages utilize structure-dependant operations (e.g. interrogatives are formed from indicatives on the basis of the latter's phrase structure, and not by, say, mere change in word order).

    ii.   Grammatical rules are constrained by the so-called 'A-over-A' principle (i.e. any transformation rule applicable to phrases of type X must, where the phrase contains another phrase of type X as a part, operate upon the whole phrases before operating on the contained one. (See Chomsky 1968 : pp. 43ff)).

(i. and ii. are examples of what Chomsky calls 'formal' universals — principles which determine the nature, and manner of operation, of rules in any grammar).

iii.   All sound systems utilize some sub-set out of twenty or so distinctive features of phonology.

iv.   Any sound system containing a vowel system will have contrasts of tongue height.

v.   All (or nearly all) languages have sentences of both the active and passive forms.

vi.   All languages contain morphemes.

vii.   All (or nearly all) languages contain noun-like, verb-like, and adverb-like phrases.

viii.   All (or nearly all) languages show a preference for suffixing over prefixing.

ix.   All (or nearly all) languages employ sentences of the subject/predicate form.

x.   There are ambiguous expressions in all languages.

xi.   All languages contain deictic expressions.

xii.   Each language can be used to talk about itself; that is, each permits the making of meta-linguistic statements.

xiii.   All languages are learnable.

xiv.   All languages contain words part of whose meaning is *male*.

Looking at this list, it becomes obvious first, that a finer classification of universals than one into, say, 'formal' and 'substantive' is required; second, that no one explanation is likely to account for the presence of all universals; and third, that some of the universals could not possibly invite explanation in terms of a specifically linguistic innate component. iv., presumably, simply tells us something about the human vocal apparatus, and xiv. merely shows that all humans find sexual differences worth remarking upon.

What I shall do is to look, in connection with some of the more interesting cases, at various alternatives to an 'innatist' explanation. Each alternative, I suggest, sounds more plausible than that hypothesis in certain cases; and the total of the alternatives might leave little or nothing for an innateness hypothesis to do.

First, there is the possibility that some of the features

are only linguistic universals in the rather dull sense that we would refuse to *call* any communicative system lacking them by the name 'language'. In extreme cases, the feature may be one we have included in some stipulative, though not necessarily arbitrary, definition of 'language'. More likely it would belong to a cluster of features we find useful for distinguishing some communicative systems, those that are paradigmatically languages, from others. Consider vi. for example. It is not that communication has to rely upon morphemic constituents, as opposed, say, to the continuously varying pitch found in some animal systems. Rather it is reasonable to restrict the term 'language' to those systems which do employ morphemes. From the fact that all *languages* employ morphemes, no conclusions concerning specifically innate communicative predispositions can be drawn. We have not been shown that humans could not communicate in other ways — indeed, we know that they can — but merely that these other ways are not to count as linguistic.

Second, there is the possibility of explanation in terms of the common origin of all languages. If all were descended from a single parent, it would be no cause for surprise that they should share various characteristics. Indeed, if they did not, there could be no great reason for supposing they are monogenetically descended. Given an explanation in terms of common origin, an appeal to innate factors would be otiose unless it could be shown — which it cannot — that no language of a different type could be learned.

Chomsky, however, has two disparaging things to say about the hypothesis of common origin: first, that there is no evidence for it, and second, that it could not explain what needs to be explained, namely the child's 'internalization' of universal grammar in each generation. This second point, though, is irrelevant in the present context. Even if the appeal to common origin did nothing to explain the child's 'internalization', it would still serve as an alternative account of the presence of universal features of language — and that is all that is being claimed. No doubt the question could remain of why the original language took the form it did. But the fact that a single language took the form it did — and, after all, it had to take some form — could provide no support for innateness. If it could, the whole stress that 'innatists' put upon universality would be inexplicable.

Two remarks are in place concerning Chomsky's first point, to the effect that there is no evidence for common origin. First, the normal and perhaps only evidence for supposing that a number of languages form a·significant group descended from a common source (e.g. Romance languages) are the similarities found among them. Now I do not see why evidence which is thought relevant to showing that *some* languages are derived from a common origin, namely the similarities among them, would not also be relevant to showing that *all* languages have a common origin. If it is replied that the similarities found among all languages are not sufficiently impressive to suggest this explanation, then it is not clear how they could be sufficiently impressive to suggest an explanation in terms of innate endowment either. The second remark is this: the claim that there is no evidence for common origin must mean, presumably, that there is no evidence *beyond* what is furnished by linguistic universals. This claim, I gather, is true.[6] The trouble is that there is no other evidence for innateness either, beyond the universality of features — at least, there is not if you accept the arguments of this book. Now if universals are used to establish innateness, despite the lack of other evidence, why is it not equally proper (or improper) to use universals to establish the monogenetic hypothesis? Suppose we found that the Martians spoke a language remarkably like English and French. I would be just as happy or unhappy to suppose that Martians must have had some historical contact with Earth as to suppose they have independently been through just the kind of evolutionary development we have, resulting in just our kind of innate linguistic endowment.

As a third type of alternative to 'innatist' explanations of universals, it may be that some of them can be seen as instances of *general* universals of psychology. I mean that some linguistic universals might be predictable, perhaps in unobvious ways, from what we know of human psychology in general; from, say, the nature of learning. It might well be that some of these psychological universals must be seen as reflections of something innate; but that *something* innate must play a role in bringing about behaviour, including linguistic, is a truism which, we have seen, is not at issue. What is at issue is the existence of dispositions to linguistic behaviour unrelated to, and unpredictable on the basis of, more general behavioural dispositions. In connection with this third alternative, we might look at vii.; the preference among languages for suffixing over prefixing. What might explain this? Well, first, there are considerations from general learning theory that might be brought to bear. Osgood (1949) has argued that in 'convergent' cases, where varied stimuli call forth 'functionally identical' responses, learning is facilitated (through transfer and retroactive facilitation); whereas in 'divergent' cases, in which similar stimuli elicit highly varied responses, learning is not facilitated. Now the order prefix-stem bears some analogy with the order of stimuli and responses in 'divergent' cases — a highly restricted set followed by a large, open one. Equally, the order stem-suffix bears some analogy with the 'convergent' case — a large, open set followed by a highly restricted one. If these analogies can be made out, one would expect, on the grounds of general learning theory, that learning would be facilitated in a language preferring the order stem-suffix. In that event, we would expect languages over the course of time to show a tendency towards extinction of prefixing. There might be other, more obvious, psychological considerations that are relevant. In a fairly clear sense, the stem generally plays the more important communicative role. A telegram that left out the affixes would be intelligible in a way that one leaving out the stems could not be. In the more technical language of information theory, identification of the stem, precisely because it eliminates more possibilities than identification of the affix, is the more crucial in retrieving the message. Now it is *generally* the case, inside and outside of language, that men precede the less important by the more important, spatially or temporally. Speakers will want to mention the more important first, and hearers will not want to wait around for the more important to be mentioned. And on this basis one would expect a preference for suffixing over prefixing.

Finally, and not entirely separately, one might expect the general interests men have in engaging in discourse, or the general functions of discourse, to impose similar features on the means employed. A wide-ranging group of examples might show how this is so. For instance, when a speaker mentions several things in a sentence, there is typically just one thing with which he is primarily concerned; one thing he is concerned to talk *about.* Given this, and given what we recently noted, namely the tendency to put first things first, it is hardly surprising that languages should have both active and passive forms. For if John has hit Mary, but it is Mary who interests us, we shall want some device for mentioning Mary before we mention John. Hence we say 'Mary was hit by John'. Again, functional discourse will be as brief as is compatible with a high degree of clarity. Hence we would expect languages to utilize all sorts of abbreviatory devices. We should expect, for example, that languages would permit us to say something like 'John and Harry came home', rather than 'John came home. Harry came home'.[7] There might be ubiquitous features of languages which, in deeper and more interesting ways, play abbreviatory and simplifying roles — in which case they would be predictable on general grounds of function and speakers' intelligence. Consider noun phrases — or, at any rate, those which occur in subject position referring to spatio-temporal particulars. Perhaps it is not strictly necessary for languages used by peoples recognizably like ourselves to contain means for mentioning such particulars, or at least for mentioning them within the device of subject/predicate constructions. But, it is arguable, there are strong reasons why languages should be expected to.

> Given our actual situation, and given that we wish to say things having approximately the force of the things we actually do say, then the premium on the introduction of ordinary concrete particulars is enormous, the gains in simplicity overwhelming (Strawson 1959 : p. 225).

Nouns for particulars are made possible by, and reflect, principles for identifying, distinguishing, and reidentifying items in our experience. 'This man', 'that man', or 'another man' are usable precisely because there are criteria for identifying and reidentifying spatio-temporal instances of a 'sortal' concept. Now perhaps it is possible to do something analogous to identifying and reidentifying without the notion of basic particulars; but there is no reason to think this could be easy. A language, for example, which allowed us, simply, to remark on the similarities between features encountered today and features encountered yesterday, would leave no room for the crucial distinction we make between similarity and numerical identity. If there is a premium on having the means for mentioning particulars, it would also seem there is an economy in having the relevant expressions occur in subject position. Except in one's moments as a professional logician, one would obviously prefer 'The man is smiling' over 'There is one and only one x such that x is a man and is smiling'.[8] Clearly, we are getting into deep questions, which I do not want to pursue. But the possibilities raised are surely ones that would have to be examined before hasty conclusions about linguistic innateness, as opposed to general factors of function and intelligence, as the source of universal features of language are drawn.

The above remarks are not meant to be conclusive. Some of them rest on empirical guesses that would have to be confirmed through further investigation. They were made, rather, with the intention of showing that there are alternatives, none of them intrinsically implausible, to an innateness hypothesis for explaining the more interesting linguistic universals. Lyons has said that Chomsky's case for innateness is 'not proven'. As things stand, I rather doubt that it would get taken into court — not, at least, in a place where innocence is presumed.

So far, we have been assuming that there are such things as linguistic universals to explain — ones, that is, of a fairly interesting kind. I now want to make some remarks, of a broadly methodological type, about this assumption.

So far, I have been using the expressions 'universal features of language' and 'universal features of a grammar' indifferently. But there is a distinction that lurks here. There are features which one discovers and observes, in a straightforward way, to belong to all languages. On one's travels one finds that no people have words that would take five minutes to utter. These are universals of language. But when we turn to a universal like deep structure, it is more perspicuous to regard it as a notion that figures in a grammatical theory applicable to each and every language. Deep structures, so to speak, have their *esse* in the theory used to describe utterances, not in the sentences themselves. The only sense I can lend to the claim that sentences contain both deep and surface features is that the grammar of the language provides different representations for the sentences. The sentence no more contains a deep structure than a polychromatic painting contains the black lines that an art historian might employ in a model for analysing structural aspects of the painting. No doubt we could take more literally this talk of sentences containing deep structures if we accepted the view that these structures are 'mentally represented' by those uttering the sentences – but we do not.

I raise this point in order to draw attention to what might be meant by 'discovering' or 'finding out' that certain features are linguistic universals. What could be meant, in many cases, is only that a grammar found adequate for describing some language is discovered to contain features adequate for describing all languages. But is there a real *discovery* here? The problem is this: there is no doubt that the grammarian might have begun with a different grammar for the original language, and that some of the features in this could have been incorporated into the grammars for all languages. So it looks as if what features turn out to be universal is going to depend upon what grammar he opted for to describe the first language. But this makes it strange to speak of his discovering universal features. If we did speak in this way, we should have to say he had *failed* to discover an indefinite number of universals – since there are an indefinite number of alternative grammars he might have started with, containing features that could be incorporated into the grammars for all languages. Suppose, for example, you start with a Chomskyan grammar of English, in which subjects are understood in terms of configurations of underlying constituents: Subject = df.

leftmost NP in the underlying structure. You might find it none too hard to 'discover' subjects in all languages, for even where there do not seem to be any, you can insist that there are; it is just that they have been 'deleted' in the surface forms of sentences. But suppose, instead, you had begun with a 'case' grammar for English, like Fillmore's, in which the subject/predicate construction is seen as a superficial reflection at the level of word order of underlying case relations — relations, say, between Agentives and Locatives. In that event, you would not have the same motivation for finding subject/ predicate constructions in all languages. Where the native sentences do not seem, at the level of surface structure, to have subjects, then they *do not* have subjects. For subjects are obvious and superficial phenomena. Or, to hark back to something mentioned earlier (p. 108), has Ross *discovered* that all sentences have the form 'I V . . . . ' (where V is some illocutionary verb)? Of course not. He is imposing, perhaps wisely, a certain analysis upon all sentences.

Before considering any implications for innateness, let us press on with a second consideration. Someone might say that even if one's list of universals is not determined by objective discovery, and rests upon initial preferences, it is still impressive that features employed in the grammar for one language can be incorporated into the grammars for all languages. So there must be basic similarities between languages, even if there is some freedom in how we list them. But is this any more impressive than the fact that all languages are, more or less, mutually translatable? And is this any more impressive than the fact that all men display regularities in their linguistic and non-linguistic behaviour? And is this to say any more than that all men have languages? Let me try to trace the suggested connections here. If a people is to be credited with understanding a language — with a communicative system intelligible among them — then, by previous arguments, they must have dispositions to regular behaviour; to, say, regularly producing certain noises in the presence of things of a certain kind. Where men do not share these dispositions towards verbal behaviour, there is no linguistic community, no shared system of communication embodied in their noises. Now if these people are at all like ourselves, they will be faced by things and situations similar to those faced by us, and they will have ways of describing or otherwise verbally responding to them. But if so, their language must be translatable, however roughly, into our own, and vice-versa. For translation, or the beginning of translation, *is* the pairing of utterances (ours with theirs) made in suitably similar situations. If we can make any sense of a people — if their behaviour is at all regular, and regular in ways isomorphic to our own to some degree — translation can, and must be able to, begin. So where there is another language, there is a scheme for translating it into our own. But with translatability, there comes the guarantee of describing the native language in at least some of the terms we use to describe our own. Translate the native sentence as 'It is raining', and you have guaranteed they use something like verbs.

Someone might say: what is remarkable is not that native sentences can be paired with *some* sentences that can be concocted in English, but with nice, ordinary, basic English sentences; and it is not just whole native sentences that can be paired with English sentences, but bits of native sentences with bits of English ones — so there must be basic similarities, including structural ones, between the two languages. This comment takes us back to the *motif* of the last chapter. Of course, one can translate the native sentence as the nice, ordinary 'That is a dog', but one could equally translate it as the far from nice or ordinary 'Now it is dogging' or 'Thither a lump of dogium'. And if we did the latter, the impressive similarities between the languages would evaporate. Naturally we shall prefer to translate into the nice, ordinary sentences. Why, after all, would one prefer the tortuous ones? But this does not mean the ordinary translations are correct in a way the tortuous ones are not. Correctness is no more decidable here than in the cases of Pierre and Peter (though see note 9 to chapter 8). If the tortuous translations are unacceptable, and in that sense 'incorrect', it is precisely for that reason — their tortuousness.

This second consideration, about the imposition of universals through translation, is not dependant on the first one, about the selection of universals depending on an initial preference among grammars for one's own language. Suppose, for example, subjects and predicates are not understood in Chomsky's way (see p. 176), but semantically — in terms of their referential and descriptive roles. In that case, there is no doubt that English contains as a basic feature, subject/predicate constructions. But that would not alter the fact that objective tests for the presence of the construction in other languages are missing. As Quine, from whom my second consideration obviously borrows, says:[9]

> Point . . . in those languages to the translations of the English subject/predicate construction, and you establish the thesis: the subject/predicate construction occurs in all those languages. Or is it imposed by translation? What is the difference? Does the thesis say more than that basic English is translatable into all those languages? And what does even this latter claim amount to, pending some standard of faithfulness and objectivity of translation? (1970 : p. 390).

The two considerations can be taken together, though, and when this is done there are some dampening implications for the innateness hypothesis. I am not denying there are linguistic universals, including those I referred to as 'universal features of grammar'. That is, I am not denying that features employed in a grammar for one language may be exported into the grammars for all languages. But I do deny that universals arrived at in the ways described over the last few pages could call for, or faintly suggest, explanation in terms of specifically linguistic innate factors. The objective discovery (whatever that might be) of significant features belonging to each and every language might at least make 'innatist' explanations appropriate, even if false. But if the 'existence' of the universals depends, first, on an undetermined preference for one out of an indefinite number of grammars for one's own language, and second, on the unsurprising fact of translatability (of non-tortuous kinds), then any appeal to innateness is out of place. One cannot regard the universal F as a reflection of innate structure if, with different grammatical preferences, and different translational aims in mind, F would not figure on a list of universals at all. Put crudely: universals depend upon choice, while what is innate does not.

My final methodological remarks also concern the status of universals, and lead to the same conclusion — that their status is not such as to make 'innatist' explanations appropriate, let alone tempting. For Chomsky, Katz, and others, linguistic universals are 'mentally represented'; they have 'psychological reality'. This objectionable view, I said (pp. 161 ff), is not strictly necessary to the claim that universals are evidence for innateness. But it does, I suggest, make universals sound far more apt than they in fact are for explanation in terms of innateness.

Let us concentrate on what, for Chomsky, is the most significant universal of them all — structure-dependence. All languages, it appears, utilize structure-dependant operations. Interrogatives, for examples, are never related to indicatives simply by a regular permutation of word order, or by the insertion of a particular interrogative morpheme or sound. Always there is a basic preservation of the indicative's phrase structure. For Chomsky, it is 'human language' which utilizes such operations; it is speakers themselves who derive one kind of sentence from another kind by structure-dependent transformations. But such a view, given the arguments of this book, is untenable. That speakers utter interrogatives which are related to indicatives by operations specified by grammarians need not be denied. But that the speakers themselves perform these operations, that they know that the operations are of a certain sort, does need to be denied. I shall not repeat my objections to the above view, for my present concern is with the impression it creates concerning the nature of universals and their psychological implications. Accept such a view and you have the picture of all speakers, the world over, engaging in fundamentally similar mental activities and processes (*deriving* sentences from others; *employing* rules, etc.). You will then conclude, pretty quickly, that such activities and processes form part of men's innate intellectual apparatus.

But suppose this myth of mental activities and processes

is seen for what it is. What does the universality of structure-dependence then show us? Only this: that in all languages, when people ask questions, issue commands, or speak in conditionals, certain phrases or groups of words are kept intact, as they occur in the corresponding indicative sentences. For example, one asks 'Is the fat man smiling?', so preserving intact the expression 'the fat man' as it appears in the indicative 'The fat man is smiling'. And, so I am told, one finds something similar happening in all languages. But that is all one finds. Beyond this, each language will have its own idiosyncratic means for asking questions, or issuing commands. Perhaps this phenomenon of structure-dependence is important and interesting. What I do not see is that it should occasion surprise, or send us off in search of deep explanations. If you are interested in the fat man, and have an expression for referring to him (i.e. 'the fat man') it would seem to me only natural that this expression should remain unbroken whether one is describing the man, asking something about him, telling someone to do something about him, or whatever. It would be no more surprising than the fact that if you are asked to draw someone's head then you will, unless you are a Picasso or Braque, put the marks standing for the eyes, ears, nose, etc. fairly close together, and not scattered about in opposite corners of the paper. Of course one *could* represent heads by having the mark for the nose over here, and the mark for the mouth over there in a different corner — but it is the methods of Picasso and Braque that require an effort of understanding on our part, not the ordinary methods. I suggest that we find in structure-dependence, then, an entirely natural, general, and predictable phenomenon. (What I have said would not, of course, explain why we do not ask questions, say, by simply adding a certain interrogative noise to the indicative. Such a method, though, by relying upon the vagaries of human vocal apparati and surrounding noises, would lead to frequent misunderstandings. Having words in a different order will be extra insurance against confusing the statement with the question).

The preceding remarks are not unrelated to the first two considerations, nor to my criticisms of KLT. If grammars

181

were 'known', 'mentally represented', or 'internalized' by speakers then, first, there would be a single 'correct' choice of a grammar for one's own language; and second, exportation of features in this grammar into grammars for other languages would be objectively determinable. In that case my earlier considerations would not have the force I imagined. But since KLT is false, they do have that force. I said earlier that the argument from universals for innateness did not presuppose KLT. But we can now see that unless KLT is accepted, universals (of an interesting type) will not have the status that would make 'innatist' explanations appropriate.

Notes to chapter 9

1. See Yolton for these and other passages from 17th C. authors.
2. See Stich (1972) for detailed criticism along these lines.
3. See Greenberg, Osgood & Jenkins (p. xix f).
4. That is, real children do not discourse on geometry or politics within minutes of being born.
5. See Osgood (1963).
6. See Greenberg (1957).
7. See Putnam.
8. Bach has, I think, argued that all nouns originate in predicate positions, and get moved to subject positions for reasons of economy.
9. Quine, in fact, overstates the case to the extent of ignoring those universals which can be objectively discovered — e.g. the absence of words which would take five minutes to utter. But, as the example suggests, these universals are not likely to excite.

Chapter 10

Grammar and
Psychology

In this final chapter I do not intend to add anything of substance but, rather, to employ earlier conclusions in reflecting on the relationship between grammatical theory and psychology. Linguistics, Chomsky has said, is a sub-field of psychology; and, as we have seen, a grammar for a proponent of KLT is nothing short of a statement of the principles and categories that constitute a vital part of our intellectual apparatus.

It would be easy to let the question 'Is grammar psychology?' degenerate into an uninteresting verbal question, answerable in as many ways as there are predilections for how to define 'psychology'. I do not want to let this happen, and am not overconcerned with what the definition of 'psychology', if there is one, might be. Rather I shall look at the various senses that, in the most liberal spirit, this term might be allowed to bear. I shall then argue, in keeping with earlier conclusions, that grammar is psychology only in the most dull and modest of the senses allowed. There will be those who would deny that some of my senses are genuine ones, and who would therefore — assuming they accept my arguments — deny that grammar can count as psychology in any sense. Such an attitude is congenial enough to me. I regard it as a matter of indifference whether we deny that grammar is psychology, or admit that it is but only in the most boring of senses. But, to scotch accusations of overnarrow definition, I shall proceed to allow 'psychology' the widest possible range of senses.

Naturally, the denial that grammar is, in any interesting

sense, a branch of psychology, does not entail that acceptance of a grammar will not have important and obvious implications for descriptions of the human mind. Chromatology, considered as the theory of the physical nature of colours, is not a psychological theory, but any description of colour perception is bound to take note of chromatological discoveries. For whatever our perceptual powers may be, they are those which operate upon the physical phenomena as described in an adequate chromatology. Equally, whatever the nature of the mental powers involved in speaking a language, they are those which allow for the production and understanding of sentences as described by an acceptable grammar for the language. Languages, moreover, are learned; so, whatever the nature of human learning might be, it is of a sort which results in speaking a language as describable by an adequate grammar. Trivially, then, acceptance of some grammar will rebound on how we characterize the nature of mind or learning. If that is all we mean by calling grammar 'psychology', so be it!

On several occasions, we have had cause to mention that the grammarian's data necessarily include psychological phenomena — judgments about acceptability, intuitions about ambiguity, 'bizarreness' reactions, and so on. An adequate grammar, that is, could not be constructed on the basis merely of an observed corpus of speech, however long. People often speak ungrammatically, and, what is more, know they do. So, if a theory is a psychological one whenever its data include psychological phenomena then, in this sense, grammar is psychology. But two dampening remarks are in order here. First, the grammarian's data are by no means exclusively psychological. Everyday, unreflective speech may be insufficient to determine the shape of a grammar, but it is crucial nonetheless and in some instances may be taken to override speakers' judgments about their speech. (For example, I should think a grammarian is quite entitled to ignore the oft-heard judgment that split infinitives are ungrammatical. They are regularly produced; except among the pedantic they do not invite immediate criticism; they do not affect intelligibility — and so on). Other data, beyond speakers' judgments, are fair game for the grammarian too — stress phenomena, for instance, or comparison with foreign languages. Second, there are in any number of areas theories and descriptions the data for which include men's beliefs, judgments, or feelings, but which are not thought, for that reason, to be psychological theories or descriptions. Consider, say, an attempt to codify the rules of etiquette operating within some community or country. The data are bound to include participants' beliefs as to what is polite, impolite, 'U', or 'non-U'. Mere observation of stretches of dinner-table behaviour will not suffice. Or consider a theory of common law. The data here must comprise judgments (in a very literal sense), beliefs, attitudes, and intentions of magistrates, judges, and others. Yet manuals on etiquette or common law are not, in any useful sense, manuals of psychology.

Someone might claim, more strongly, that a grammar is actually a description of psychological phenomena — of intuitive judgments, for example — and not merely a set of descriptions for which such phenomena provide crucial data. Even Stich who is as hostile as myself towards KLT, writes:

> . . . a grammar is a modest portion of a psychological theory about the speaker. It describes certain language-specific facts: facts about the acceptability of expressions to speakers and facts about an ability or capacity speakers have for judging and classifying expressions as having or lacking grammatical properties and relations (1972 : p. 816).

I agree that if grammar did this it would still only be a *modest* portion of psychological theory. Merely to describe a speaker as capable of making various judgments is not to explain how he does this, nor is it to illuminate what it is he is doing. As Stich continues:

> A theory of language seriously worthy of the name would provide some insight into what it is to *understand* a sentence, how sentences can be used to communicate and to deal more effectively with the world . . . a grammar does none of this (p. 817).

However, I doubt that it is perspicuous to regard a grammar as descriptive of linguistic judgments and abilities. To begin with, while a grammar must start with the definite judgments speakers make about relatively short and simple sentences it must, if it is to remain manageably simple, go beyond speakers' judgments in at least two ways. First, its rules will provide for decisions about sentences concerning which speakers either have no definite intuitions or have definitely conflicting ones among themselves. Second, the rules will, unless they are to be arbitrary in their application, have to provide for decisions on sentences of a length and complexity which make it impossible for ordinary speakers to form judgments about. For such reasons, it could not be correct to regard a rule of grammar as a mere summary of what ordinary speakers judge. In the second place, it is easy to confuse the claim that a theory describes psychological facts with one or other of the following claims: either the previously encountered one that psychological facts are among the data warranting the description, or that various psychological facts can be inferred from it. There has for long been a tradition in the philosophy of science according to which scientific theories are essentially about the beliefs, judgments, or observations of scientists and others. You can find the tradition represented, in different ways, by Berkeley, Mach, and Collingwood. But surely this is to confuse what the theory is about — falling objects, say — with the evidential data for the theory — observations made through microscopes, for instance. (Actually, it is misleading to regard the observations as data. We should want to respect a distinction between the data — what actually happens on the glass slide — and the ways in which such data are discovered and appreciated). Or it is to confuse what the theory is about — electrons, say — with what we might expect if the theory is true, such as observing traces in cloud chambers or whatever. Now it seems to me that a grammar is about sentences, expressions, ambiguity, vocalization, and so on. To suppose it is essentially about speakers' beliefs or capacities is to muddle what it is about with what furnishes data for it or what can be inferred from it. Certainly beliefs do serve as data; and certainly, as we have seen, one can trivially infer descriptions of capacities from acceptance of a grammar. Neither admission commits us to treating a grammar as a set of descriptions of those beliefs and capacities.

A different suggestion for treating grammar as psychology might be this: a grammar indeed describes and is about sentences and expressions, but these are objects of thought, understanding, and acquaintance — and a description belongs to psychology to the extent that it deals with objects of psychological acquaintance. The trouble with this suggestion resides in the ambiguity of 'object of acquaintance (thought, understanding)'. Taken in one way a grammar does indeed describe objects of thought — but then so does nearly every theory you like to mention. Taken in another way, one which would make the claim significant, it is simply untrue that grammars of the types proposed in recent years describe objects of thought. Stones are things with which we are acquainted and about which we can think and have beliefs. So, in one sense, stones are objects of thought. Hence any description of a stone is a description of an object of psychological acquaintance. Hence, on the present suggestion, petrology must be a branch of psychology! In another sense, a notoriously difficult one, a description of an object of thought is necessarily intensional. It is, very roughly, a description of something *as* perceived, understood, thought of, or interpreted by the subject. Petrological descriptions of stones are rarely descriptions of objects of thought in this sense. This distinction, or one akin to it, is needed to characterize the very different kinds of answer there could be to a question like 'What can he see?'. Suppose a man is put before the famous duck/rabbit *gestalt* drawing. In the former of our senses any description of that drawing — mentioning, perhaps, the thickness of the ink, the molecular structure of the paper, or the name of the person who drew it — would count as a description of the object of the subject's vision. In the second of our senses, such descriptions would be out of place, whereas mention of what he sees it as (e.g. a duck) would be vital. In the first sense, the object of vision does not change when the subject's *gestalt* perception does; in the second sense, it does. Now if grammatical descriptions of sentences were intensional in nature, we could grant the significance of treating grammar as a portion of psychology —

for the descriptions would be of sentences and their properties as they are judged, understood, or analysed by speakers. But the thrust of several chapters, especially chapter 6, has been that the descriptions offered by generative grammarians are not intensional. Whatever it is that speakers intuit when they judge sentences to be ambiguous, synonymous, or related, it is not the presence of features and structures as described by the grammar. Sentences, it seems to me, are only objects of thought in the way stones are, so that grammar is psychology only if petrology is as well.

The above complete, I think, the very dull, modest, and barely permissible senses in which grammar might be treated as psychology. If so to treat it is merely to claim that psychological phenomena are among the grammarian's data, that implications may be drawn (trivially) concerning human capacities, and that grammar describes (in the non-intensional sense) objects of human acquaintance, then I have no complaints. Grammar becomes a branch of psychology; but this is a statement devoid of interest. It is apparent, too, that those who have bothered to stress the psychological status of grammar have meant to advocate something far more elevated. What they have advocated is certainly not devoid of interest. Unfortunately, it is false. Naturally, these advocates would take issue with much that I have said in this chapter. In particular, they would challenge my denials that a grammar does anything to explain linguistic abilities or tells us anything of the processes, if any, involved in speaking, interpreting, and judging. In connection with the latter, we have encountered on several occasions the extreme version of KLT proposed by Katz. For him a grammar is not merely a description of psychological processes involved in sentence production and interpretation, but of physiological ones as well.

> The linguistic description and the procedures of sentence production and recognition must correspond to independent mechanisms in the brain. . . . The rules of each component must have their psychological reality in the input-output operations of the computing machinery of this mechanism (1967 : p. 81).

Against such a view I have urged that it presupposes a totally implausible model of performance; that insufficient warrant has been provided for lending sense to the talk of unconscious processes and acts; and that there is no way in which the 'psychologically real' rules could be identified and hence significantly postulated. Chomsky, less extremely, has not insisted that a grammar is a model of linguistic performance, but he has insisted that speakers' knowledge or 'internalization' of a grammar is required to explain linguistic behaviour. This proposal suffers from the same crippling problem of the identifiability of the rules said to be known or 'internalized'. Further, I have argued, there is nothing that is explained or predicted on the assumption that speakers have 'internalized' a certain grammar that is not explained or predicted on the barer assumption that speakers are disposed to speak in accordance with the rules of that grammar. And if we make only the latter assumption then grammatical rules have no more 'psychological reality' for speakers than physical laws do for stones.

More exotic claims even than those just mentioned have been made by advocates of the psychological status of grammar. The most general grammatical rules and categories, we are told, specify universal, innate features of our mental make-up. Or the derivation of lower from higher syntactic categories in tree-diagrams represents the temporal sequence through which a child passes in refining his intellectual linguistic equipment. Such claims fall prey to the same objections as the wider and less exotic ones from which they stem.

The views mentioned in the previous two paragraphs complete, I think, the strong and interesting senses in which it could be held that a grammar is a portion of psychology. Such views are incoherent. I conclude, then, that grammar is psychology only in the dullest of senses — so dull, in fact, that the natural and least misleading reaction is to deny the status of psychology to grammar altogether.

References

Alston, W. *Philosophy of Language*. Prentice-Hall, 1964

Arbini, R. 'Comments on linguistic competence and language acquisition', *Synthese* 19 1968-9

Armstrong, D. *A Materialist Theory of Mind*, Routledge & Kegan Paul, 1968

Austin, J.L. *Philosophical Papers*, Oxford U.P. 1962

Bach, E. 'Nouns and noun phrases', in Bach & Harms (eds.) *Universals in Linguistic Theory*, Holt, Rinehart, & Winston 1968

Black, M. *Models and Metaphors*, Cornell U.P. 1962

Bloomfield, L. *Linguistic Aspects of Science*, Chicago U.P. 1944

Brown, R. *Words and Things*, Free Press 1958

Campbell, R. & Wales, R. 'The study of language acquisition', in Lyons, J. (ed.) *New Horizons in Linguistics*, Penguin 1970

Carroll, J. 'Words, meanings, and concepts', in Ewig, Flemming, and Popp (eds.) *Language and Learning*, Harcourt, Brace, and World 1966

Cavell, S. 'Must we mean what we say?', *Inquiry* 1, 1958

Chomsky, N. *Syntactic Structures*, Mouton 1957

—————— 'Review of B.F. Skinner's *Verbal Behaviour*', in Fodor & Katz (eds.) *The Structure of Language*, Prentice-Hall, 1964

—————— *Aspects of the Theory of Syntax*, M.I.T., 1965

—————— 'Recent contributions to the theory of innate ideas', *Synthese* 17, 1967

—————— *Language and Mind*, Harcourt, Brace, & World, 1968

—————— 'Quine's empirical assumptions', *Synthese* 19, 1968-9

—————— 'Linguistics and philosophy', in Hook (ed.) *Language and Philosophy*, New York U.P., 1969a

—————— 'Comments on Harman's reply', in Hook (op. cit.), 1969b

—————— 'Problems of explanation in linguistics', in Borger &

Cioffi (eds.) *Explanation in the Behavioural Sciences*, Cambridge U.P. 1970

―――― 'Deep structure, surface structure, and semantic interpretation', in Steinberg & Jakobovits (eds.) *Semantics*, 1971.

Cohen, L.J. & Margolit, A. 'The role of inductive reasoning in the interpretation of metaphor', in Davidson & Harman (eds.) *Semantics of a Natural Language*, Reidel 1972

Cooper, D.E. 'Innateness: old and new', *Philosophical Review* 81, 1972

―――― *Philosophy and the Nature of Language*, Longman's, 1973a

―――― *Presupposition*, Mouton 1973b

―――― 'Grammar and the possession of concepts', *Supp. Procs. of the Philosophy of Education Society of G.B.*, 1973c

Descartes, R. *Philosophical Works* (tr. by Haldane & Ross), Cambridge U.P., 1931

Edgley, R. 'Innate ideas', in *Knowledge and Necessity*, Royal Institute of Philosophy Lectures, MacMillan 1970

Fillmore, C. 'The case for case', in Bach & Harms (eds.) *Universals in Linguistic Theory*, Holt, Rinehart, & Winston, 1968

Fodor, J.A. 'How to learn to talk: some simple ways', in Smith & Miller (eds.) *The Genesis of Language*, M.I.T. 1966

―――― 'The appeal to tacit knowledge in psychological explanation', *Journal of Philosophy*, 65, 1968a

―――― *Psychological Explanation*, Random House, 1968b

―――― & Bever, T.G., 'The psychological reality of linguistic segments', in Jakobovits & Miron (eds.) *Readings in the Psychology of Language*, Prentice-Hall, 1967

―――― & Katz, J.J. 'The structure of a semantic theory', in Fodor & Katz (eds.) *The Structure of Language*, Prentice-Hall, 1964

Geach, P. *Mental Acts*, Routledge & Kegan Paul, 1957

Goodman, N. *Languages of Art*, Bobbs-Merrill, 1968

―――― 'The emperor's new ideas', in Hook (ed.) *Language and Philosophy*, New York U.P., 1969

Graves, C., Katz, J.J., et. al. 'Tacit knowledge', *Journal of Philosophy*, 70, 1973

Greenberg, J.H., *Essays in Linguistics*, Chicago U.P., 1957

Greenberg, J.H., Osgood, C., and Jenkins, J.: 'Memorandum concerning language universals', in Greenberg (ed.) *Universals of Language*, M.I.T., 1963

Hamlyn, D. 'Human learning', in *Philosophy of Education* (ed) R.S. Peters Oxford U.P. 1973

Harman, G. 'Psychological aspects of the theory of syntax', *Journal of Philosophy*, 64, 1967

————— 'Three levels of meaning', *Journal of Philosophy*, 65, 1968
————— 'An introduction to 'Translation and Meaning'; Chapter 2 of *Word and Object', Synthese*, 19, 1968-9a
————— 'Reply to Arbini', *Synthese*, 19, 1968-9b
Hintikka, J. 'Behavioral criteria of radical translation', *Synthese*, 19, 1968-9
Hinton, J. *Experiences* Oxford U.P. 1973
Hiz, H. 'Methodological aspects of the theory of syntax', *Journal of Philosophy*, 64, 1967
Hume, D. *Philosophical Works*, vol. IV, Edinburgh 1826
Katz, J.J. *The Philosophy of Language*, Harper & Row, 1966
————— 'Mentalism in linguistics', in Jakobovits & Miron, (eds.) *Readings in the Psychology of Language*, Prentice-Hall, 1967
————— *Linguistic Philosophy*, Allen & Unwin, 1972
Kiparsky, P. 'Linguistic universals and linguistic change', in Bach & Harms (eds.) *Universals in Linguistic Theory*, Holt, Rinehart, & Winston, 1968
Kripke, S. 'Naming and necessity', in Davidson & Harman (eds.) *Semantics of a Natural Language*, Reidel, 1972
Lakoff, G. 'On generative semantics', in Steinberg & Jakobovits (eds.) *Semantics*, Cambridge U.P., 1971
Leibniz, G. *New Essays on Human Understanding*, (trans. A. Langley), Open Court
Lenneberg, E. *Biological Foundations of Language*, Wiley 1967
Lewis, D. *Convention*, Harvard U.P., 1969
Locke, J. *An Essay Concerning Human Understanding*, Oxford U.P., 1934
Lyons, J. *Chomsky*, Fontana, 1970
McNeill, D. 'Developmental psycholinguistics', in Smith & Miller (eds.) *The Genesis of Language*, M.I.T., 1966
————— *The Acquisition of Language*, Harper & Row, 1970
Malcolm, N. 'The myth of cognitive processes and structures', in Mischel (ed.) *Cognitive Development and Epistemology*, Academic Press, 1971
Mates, B. On the verification of statements about ordinary language', *Inquiry*, 1, 1958
Naess, A. *Interpretation and Preciseness : A Contribution to the Theory of Communication*, Oslo, 1953
Nagel, T. 'Linguistics and epistemology', in Hook (ed.) *Language and Philosophy*, New York U.P., 1969
Osgood, C. 'The similarity paradox in human learning: a resolution', *Psychological Review*, 56, 1949
————— 'Language universals and psycholinguistics', in Greenberg

193

(ed.) *Universals of Language*, M.I.T., 1963

Postal, P. 'Limitations of phrase structure grammars', in Fodor & Katz (eds.) *The Structure of Language*, Prentice-Hall, 1964

Putnam, H. 'The 'innateness hypothesis' and explanatory models in linguistics', *Synthese*, 17, 1967

Quine, W.V. *Word and Object*, M.I.T., 1960
—— *Ontological Theory Relativity*, Columbia U.P., 1969
—— 'Methodological reflections on current linguistic theory', *Synthese*, 21, 1970

Ross, J.R. 'On declarative sentences', in Jacobs & Rosenbaum (eds.) *Readings in English Transformational Grammar*, Blaisdell, 1970

Ryle, G. *The Concept of Mind*, Penguin 1963

Sanders, G. & Tai, J. 'Immediate dominance and identity deletion', *Foundations of Language*, 8, 1972

Schwartz, R. 'Review of Bruner et. al., *Studies in Cognitive Growth*', *Journal of Philosophy*, 65, 1968
—— 'On knowing a grammar', in Hook (ed.) *Language and Philosophy*, New York U.P., 1969

Searle, J.R. *Speech Acts*, Cambridge U.P., 1969

Skinner, B.F. *Verbal Behavior*, Appleton-Century-Crofts, 1957

Slobin, D.I. *Psycholinguistics*, Scott, Foresman, & Co., 1971

Smart, J.J.C. *Philosophy and Scientific Realism*, Routledge & Kegan Paul, 1963

Snyder, A. 'Rules of language', (personal copy)

Stich, S. 'What every speaker knows', *Philosophical Review*, 80, 1971
—— 'Grammar, psychology, and indeterminacy', *Journal of Philosophy*, 69, 1972

Strawson, P.F. *Individuals*, Methuen, 1959

Unger, P. 'On experience and the development of the understanding', *American Philosophical Quarterly*, 3, 1966

Vendler, Z. *Res Cogitans : An Essay in Rationalist Psychology*, Cornell U.P., 1972

Waismann, F. *The Principles of Linguistic Philosophy*, MacMillan, 1965

Wheatley, J. *Language and Rules*, Mouton, 1970

Wittgenstein, L. *Philosophical Investigations*, MacMillan, 1969
—— *On Certainty*, Blackwell's, 1969

Yolton, J.T. *John Locke and the Way of Ideas*, Oxford U.P., 1956

Ziff, P. *Semantic Analysis*, Cornell U.P., 1966
—— 'The Number of English Sentences', *Foundations of Language II*, 1974

Index of Names